Exploring Ho
Bo

Book 2

◇

Exploring Home Economics

Ruth Riddell, Lorraine Scott,
Elaine Prisk, Lynn Rogers and Miriam Staddon

Unwin Hyman

Published by
UNWIN HYMAN LIMITED
15/17 Broadwick Street
London W1V 1FP

© Ruth Riddell, Lorraine Scott, Elaine Prisk,
Lynn Rogers and Miriam Staddon

First published in 1985 by
Longman Cheshire Pty Limited

UK adaptation published in 1988 by
Unwin Hyman Limited

British Library cataloguing in Publication Data
Riddell, Ruth
    Exploring home economics.
    Book 2
    1. Home economics—For schools
    I. Title
    640

ISBN 0 7135 2793–5

Printed in Great Britain by The Alden Press, Oxford

Contents

Acknowledgements

We would like to thank the following for permission to reproduce copyright material:

Jenny Webb of the Electricity Council for length of recommended freezer storage (page 55); Methuen Australia for the diagram, 'Surface area to volume ratio' from *Food and Nutrition in Australia* by Mark L Wahlqvist (1981) (page 82); Australian Nutrition Foundation for the illustration of 'The Healthy Diet Pyramid' (page 86); *DHSS Recommended Daily Amounts of food energy and nutrients for groups of people in the UK* (HMSO 1979) (page 91–95); National Advisory Committee on Nutrition Education (NACNE report), Health Education Council 1983, for table of 'Acceptable weights' (page 96); McCance and Widdowson's *The Composition of Foods* by A A Paul and D A T Southgate (1978) for food composition figures (in many places throughout in the book).

Preface

THIS BOOK is designed to meet the needs of middle secondary school (Years 3 and 4) Home Economics. Emphasis is placed on Investigations, many food-based, which allow pupils to explore the various facets of Home Economics. It aims to develop in pupils abilities to apply their knowledge to given situations, evaluate their findings and generalise from their findings. Activities have been selected for the wide range of experiences they offer.

Exploring Home Economics Book 2 is designed either to form the basis of a middle secondary school course or fit readily into the shorter unit courses which are offered in many schools. The four parts, Resources and Me, Finding Out About Food Needs, Finding Out About Food and Finding Out About Shelter, readily form the basis of possible short-term unit courses.

Recipes have been selected to meet the preferences of the multi-cultural nature of our community. All recipes and food activities have been selected keeping in mind the dietary guidelies and the Healthy Diet Pyramid. Investigations have been developed to give pupils experiences in methods that will assist them with further studies in Home Economics.

Finding Out About Home Economics

What is Home Economics?

Most of you will have some ideas about the type of work you will do in Home Economics. Let us find out what you know. To do this we are going to conduct a class survey.

Surveys are used to find out about people: their opinions, their views, their needs, their attitudes. They may be used to find out about people in the past, present, or to help plan for the future. Some examples of surveys are:

- Rating surveys (What television programmes do you watch?)
- Transport surveys (How do you get home from work?)
- Marketing surveys (What type of food do you buy?)

In this exercise we are interested in finding out what people think the study of Home Economics involves.

Investigation No. 1
Class Survey

Aim

- The aim of this survey is to find out what your class believes Home Economics is about and to compare this with the definition of Home Economics used in GCSE courses:

  Home Economics is a study of the inter- relationships between the provision of food, clothing, shelter and related services, and man's physical, economic, social and aesthetic needs in the context of the home.

Procedure

a The first step in any survey is to select the group of people who will make up your **sample**. Your sample will represent those people relevant to the survey. (If you want to find out what a batch of scones is like, you sample one or two — this tells you what the whole batch is like. If you want to know what a large group of people think, you ask a **sample** of the group. If a group is small enough, for example your Home Economics class, then you can use the whole group as the sample.)

b Plan the questions you are going to ask. For example, list a number of school-related topics and ask the **subjects** (that is, those students making up your sample) to tick the topics related to Home Economics. Leave room for the subjects to add topics.

c Decide how the answers to the questions on your survey questionnaire can be compiled or collated (this is the presentation of the **data**). *Example:*

Area of study	No. of times mentioned	% of sample
Food		
Family		
Nutrition		
Management of resources		
Environment		
Human growth		
Health		
Housing		

d Conduct survey.

e Put answers together, that is, collate data.

f Discuss your findings (steps 'f' and 'g' are **analysis** of the data).

g Compose a definition of Home Economics from the data collected and compare this with the given definition of Home Economics.
— In what ways are they similar?
— In what ways do they differ?
— Can you give reasons for the variations?
— Discuss your results. Do the results represent the views of the whole school?

h Draw your conclusions. Did you achieve your goal/aim?

i What are the implications of your research? Does the Home Economics department need to promote what the subject is about more thoroughly? How could they do this?

Part 1

$\diamond$

Resources and Me

1 Finding Out About Me

What Do I Need to Live?

- In your own words, list all the things you believe you need to live. Number them in order of importance to you. Compare your answers with those of the person next to you. Draw up a list of needs, in order of importance for survival, with which you both agree.
- Join with another pair to make a group of four and again compare your lists of needs. As a group, draw up a list of needs, in order of importance, with which you all agree.
- Repeat the previous step with a group of eight people.
- Select a person from each group of eight to write the group's list on the board.
- As a class, come to some agreement on a priority list of needs for an individual.

What did you find out in the exercise above? Did your class mention these needs: air, water, food, shelter, clothing, love, affection, security, sleep, exercise, safety?

The needs at the top of your list (such as air, water, food, shelter) are your **basic** or **primary needs**. They are the things you need in order to stay alive.

When needs such as love and affection are met, we feel happy and contented — a whole person. These **secondary needs** are often met in our family, or in our community.

- Discuss: Why do studies in Home Economics focus so much on food, clothing, shelter and family?

Meeting Needs and Wants

People spend a lot of their time and energy in meeting the needs and satisfying the desires or wants of themselves and their families.

- Think about the reasons for your day-to-day activities. How many of them relate back to your wants and needs? What is the difference between a need and a want?

It is through satisfying our needs and wants that we achieve our quality of life.

What Do You Want to Achieve in Your Lifetime?

List all the things you would like to do and achieve in your lifetime.

These are your **aims** or **goals** in life. Striving to achieve these goals will influence what you do with your life and how you will spend your time and energies.

Alongside each of your goals indicate if it is a goal that you can achieve within

- the next week or month — a **short-term goal**
- the next three or four years — an **intermediate** or **medium-term goal**
- ten, twelve or more years — a **long-term goal**.

Some goals are more important to us than others. As we cannot achieve all our goals at once, we put them in some order, usually based on how important they are to us; that is, we give them *priorities*.

Look at the goals you have written down for yourself. Rank them in order of importance to you.

What Influences the Goals You Set?

The goals that you set for yourself will be influenced by the **values** you hold. Values are the beliefs you hold about what is important to you. You learn and develop them as part of your growing-up process. They are related to your family, religion, culture. Honesty, knowledge and love are values. For example, honesty is demonstrated in behaviour when you own up to breaking a window at school and are prepared to take the consequence for your actions. It shows that you care what other people think of you and that you are not prepared to be dishonest about what happened. You *decided* to tell the truth and take the consequences.

We learn values from each other and from the way events affect us. Our early childhood is the most important time in our lives as far as learning values is concerned. When we are young, we learn by imitating others. The most likely people for us to learn from are those in our family. Values such as love (for others, for things), neatness and honesty, if taught to us by our family in the first three or four years of our lives, will remain with us for a very long time, if not for ever.

Our values control the decisions we make.

- Look at a daily paper and see if you can identify one value held by a person mentioned in a story on the front page.

The achievement of the goals you set will also be influenced by the **resources** you have to achieve them. Resources include money, time, energy, skills and other people. They are what you use to achieve your goals. Some resources change when used, some are lost forever and some remain the same. You will understand this if you work your way through Investigation No. 2 on page 5.

Achieving My Goals

How well you achieve your goals will be influenced by the **standards** that you set for yourself. Standards are the guides used to measure success in achieving a goal. For example, a student at school may aim to get an A for homework. The assessment the student obtains could be used as a measure of how well the goal was achieved.

How Do We Decide Which Goal is More Important than Another?

Every day of our lives we have to make decisions about many things. We have to choose between alternatives to solve problems.

Decision-making

The following steps may help you to understand how decisions are made.

1 Clearly state the problem. For example, *I want to buy a radio/cassette recorder.* (**Note:** A 'problem' is not necessarily something unpleasant, it is something to be done.)

2 Collect information about the problem and possible solutions. For example, brand names, costs and access to shops.

3 Think of possible solutions to the problem. For example, I can pay a deposit so that the shop will keep it for me. Then I can work to raise the money.

4 Think about the consequences of each solution. For example, if I buy it, I won't be able to afford new jeans or I will want more money to buy tapes.

5 Select what seems the best course of action.

6 Carry it out.

3

7 Ask yourself if it was successful. If not, why
not, and what can be done? If so, why?
(This is called *evaluating* your decision.)
The following diagram might help you to
understand this a little better.

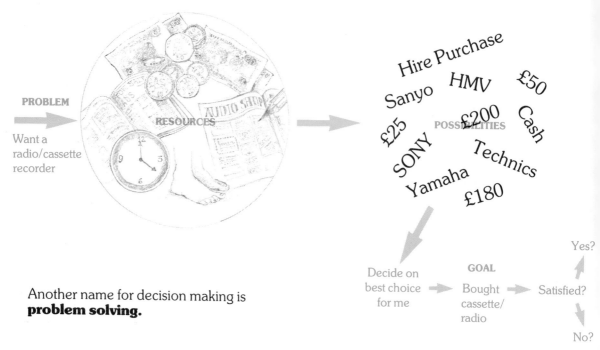

PROBLEM

Want a
radio/cassette
recorder

RESOURCES

Hire Purchase

Sanyo   HMV   £50

£25   POSSIBILITIES   Cash

SONY   £200

Yamaha   Technics

£180

Decide on
best choice
for me

GOAL

Bought
cassette/
radio

Satisfied?

Yes?

No?

Another name for decision making is
problem solving.

Workshop

1 Complete the following sentences in your book.
  a The aim of Home Economics is ...
  b A **need** is ...
  c A **want** is ...
  d A **goal** is ...
  e A **value** is ...
  f **Resources** are ...
  g **Decision-making** is ...

2 Listed below are some items often purchased by teenagers. Decide whether
each item is a need or a want. Write the heading 'Needs and Wants' in your
book and list the following items under the appropriate headings:
  Lunch   Jeans   Hair gel
  Tickets for the cinema   School stationery   Chocolate

3 Tony and Tim share a flat. They both attend the local polytechnic.
Tony is keen to do well in his studies as he wishes to become a food
technologist. Tim is not sure what he wants to do for a living and
spends most of his time socialising. At present, Tim and Tony are not

on good terms with each other. This is because Tony wants to study in the evenings and Tim wants to socialise.
a What is Tony's long-term goal?
b What is Tim's short-term goal?
c What is Tony's short-term goal?
d What is the reason for their present disagreement?
e What are some ways this problem could be solved?
f How would you solve the problem?
If you set up a role-play situation in class and act out Tony's and Tim's problems, you might find it easier to come up with possible solutions to their problem.

4 Gary and Vishna are to stay on a deserted island for two weeks as part of a survival experiment. The island has fresh water and there are plenty of fish in the sea waters that surround it. They are allowed to take ten items with them. What should they take? Discuss and come to some agreement as a group. Give reasons for your answers.

5 What is the possible *value* held in each situation below?
a Frank and Ros are brother and sister who share a common interest in music. They have many records by popular singers. They do not borrow records from one another.
b John receives a weekly allowance of £8. He spends half his allowance on books.
c Anne has gained 5 kilograms during the winter. She decides to do something about it, so she will be fit for athletics training.

Investigation No. 2
Management

Aim
- To examine the management processes involved in carrying out a task.

Procedure
a Record the time at which you start the collection of the ingredients to make up the pizza recipe on page 6.
b Make up the pizza.
c Record the time when your pizza is cooked and you have cleaned up your unit.
d Complete the following.
— What were the goals in this exercise?
— List the resources needed to complete this exercise.
— Which resources were the same before *and* after the exercise?
— Which resources could not be used again after the exercise?

— Which resources had changed their structure by the end of the exercise?
— Which resources adopted a new function after the exercise?
— Which resources could have been swapped for an alternative?
— Classify the resources used to make the pizza under the following headings:

Human resources (e.g. skills); Non-human resources (e.g. pizza tray); Renewable resources (e.g. ingredients); Non-renewable resources (e.g. time); Can be substituted (e.g. ham for salami).

— What decisions did you have to make during the exercise?
— What influenced the decisions you made during this exercise?
— Which of your basic needs did the pizza satisfy?
— What other needs were met in the process of making your pizza?
— How could you have economised on time during the exercise?
— How successful was your pizza?
— What personal standards did you use to judge the success of your pizza?

Recipe to Try

Pizza

Ingredients

120 g S.R. flour
1 tsp milk powder
1 tbsp oil
2 tbsp tomato puree
½ tsp oregano
70 ml water

Topping

choose from:
ham, salami, pineapple, cheddar or mozzarella cheese, olives, mushrooms, sardines, anchovies

Method

1 Collect ingredients, set oven to 220°C, gas mark 7.
2 Sift flour and milk powder. Mix to a soft dough with oil and water added all at once.
3 Knead gently.
4 Lightly grease pizza tray with a little oil.
5 Roll out the dough to fit the tray.
6 Spread with tomato puree and sprinkle with oregano.
7 Top with *your* selection of topping ingredients.
8 Bake 15–20 minutes until the base is cooked and the cheese has melted.
9 Clean your unit.

Research

a Calculate the cost of your pizza. Find out the cost of a similar take-away pizza. Find out the cost of a similar frozen pizza. Compare the three costs.

b What contributes to the greater cost of the commercial pizzas?

2 Finding Out About Resources

Resources are essential for us to achieve the goals that we set for ourselves. The way we manage these resources will effect the achievement of set goals.

Most resources are not unlimited and the amounts available for use will vary from person to person. Time is perhaps the only resource that we all have in an equal amount.

- What resources do you have? Make a list in your book. Compare these with the person next to you. Do your resources differ?

You may not even be aware of the resources you have. Did you consider yourself and your family as resources?

Being aware of the resources that we have and learning how to use these resources are important parts of life. We are often very wasteful of our resources. Many of the activities you will do in this section are concerned with making you aware of your resources and how to use them economically. The particular resources studied are: myself, my family, time, money and food.

Myself as a Resource

The two most important elements that make you a useful resource to yourself are:

- your ability to communicate with others;
- the way you are to others. The following activities will help you to understand this.

Workshop

1　a　Under test conditions, write in your book the meaning of the following words or statements.
　　　— 'it is flexible'
　　　— 'order them'
　　　— 'handle'
　　　— 'class'
　　b　When everyone has finished, record the answers on the board. Were they all the same? If not why not? What does this tell you about the use of words when communicating with others?

2　Each class member should be given a 'What am I?' or a 'What am I doing' card. Your card will tell you what you are or what you are doing, for example, a packet of jelly, a shoe lace, a washing machine, making a cup of tea, changing the oil in a car. Convey a message to the class by describing what you are without using the words underlined on your card.
　　● How well did you do as:
　　— a communicator?
　　— an interpreter?

3　Prepare a five minute talk. The topic can be of your own choosing or selected by your teacher. Practice it and present it to the class at the next lesson.
　　● Will you feel more confident next time you need to make a speech?

4　Look at the pictures of young people on page 9. Write a sentence describing your reactions to each person.

5　List ten characteristics of a well-groomed person. Rate each of the people in the pictures opposite for the observable grooming characteristics (give one point for each characteristic you list).

6　Copy the table on page 10 into your book and suggest whether each of the personal characteristics listed will have a positive or negative effect on a prospective employer during a job interview.

Personal characteristic	Effect	
	Positive	Negative
Bitten nails		
Pleasant smile		
Unruly hair		
Healthy teeth		
Neat clothing		

7 a What personal values influenced your answers to questions 4, 5 and 6?

   b What personal standards influenced your answers to questions 4, 5 and 6?

   c Did anyone else influence your answers?

8 a Research the correct way to care for your teeth. If possible, arrange for a dentist to visit the class to assist with this.

   b Find out if there are real differences between expensive and cheaper brands of toothpaste.

9 a Research the best way to care for your skin and hair. If possible, arrange for an expert in these areas to visit the class to assist.

   b Find out about expensive and cheaper brands of soap and shampoo. Is there any benefit in paying more for the expensive brands?

10 a Discuss in class whether there is such a thing as *correct* clothing for special occasions such as a job interview, a wedding or a sixteenth birthday party.

   b How do you account for the differences in ideas about *correct* clothing? That is, why are people different? What influences our standards and our decisions?

11 Discuss the importance of clean clothing in relation to appearance and health.

My Family as a Resource

So far it has been mentioned that not all *families* have the same resources and that it is the *family* that has the greatest influence on the values we learn. The family, therefore, has an important influence on the goals we set and the decisions we make.

What is a Family?

A family is the group that we are born or adopted into and which supplies us with our survival needs or basic needs, and varying amounts of other needs. We live in families because it makes us feel secure, because we can experience love and because that is the way our society functions.

When all members of a family pool their resources, goals are more likely to be reached. There are very few people who can function in life without the *use* of other people as resources. In a family, there is a ready-made collection of human resources for use. There is the opportunity to experience love, happiness, security, safety and self-confidence from within a family group. A family gives its members the opportunity to develop into responsible members of the community (that is, if this is the goal of the parents for their children).

Within a family each individual has responsibilities. For example, a very young child might be given the responsibility of putting his or her own shoes away before going to bed, or may be made partly responsible for the welfare of the family dog by seeing that the dog always has a bowl of clean water. As a child gets older he or she might become responsible for some of his or her own needs and wants by taking on a paper round and earning money, some of which must be saved.

● What responsibilities do you have at home?

● How do these compare with other members in your class?

Failure on the part of one family member to assume responsibilities usually means either that the family goes without something or that another family member has to take on the responsibilities.

Workshop

1 a Conduct a discussion in class to investigate the following questions:
— What is a family?
— Why do we live in families?
— What do I do for my family?
Compile ideas for each question on four large sheets of paper. Hang these sheets of paper on a notice board.
  b Organise representatives of three generations (a grandparent or elderly citizen, a parent and a student) to conduct a class discussion on the changes seen in family function over the years.
  c List the observed changes on a large sheet of paper and hang with the other sheets on a notice board. (The original sheets can be used as material for a discussion on family changes.)

2 From what you have learnt in the activity above, list three functions of the family.

3 A story of the Johnson family is given below. Read the story and list the ways in which each family member receives from the family and the ways in which each family member gives to the family.

A Saturday Afternoon with the Johnson Family

Last Saturday afternoon, eleven-year-old Matthew Johnson took his three-year-old sister Amy across the park to visit his grandmother. It was a beautiful Autumn day and Matthew persuaded his grandmother to walk back with them, visiting the swings on the way. While the children were out, Mrs. Johnson, who has just started a course at a local college, had time to write an essay.

4 Prepare a report describing your family's possible reaction if you behaved in one or more of the following ways:
  a You did not give help when needed.
  b You were dishonest.
  c You did not treat the family with respect.
  d You did not join in family fun.
Keep the report in your diary and look at it from time to time.
5 Bring a favourite family recipe from home to your next Home Economics class and help to compile a class family recipe book.

Using Resources

Time

The resource we all have in the same amount is **time**. Time, like other resources, is used to obtain the things we need and want. The way we use time is influenced by the goals we set and the values that we hold.

Investigation No. 3
Using Time

Introduction

How you spend your time can be divided into a number of categories.
- *Goal-related time* — time spent consciously directed towards achieving a goal, for example, training for a sports team.
- *Fixed-activity time* — time spent doing things that must be done, for example an appointment with the dentist.
- *Leisure time* — time spent on activities that you enjoy doing.
- *Other time* — time that does not fit into other categories.

Aim
- To find out how I use my time

Procedure
  a Select one school day and one weekend day. (Why should you choose two days?)

---

b Design a chart to record your daily activities. For example:

Time	School Day		Weekend Day	
	Activity	Category	Activity	Category
8 a.m.				
9 a.m.				
10 a.m.				
11 a.m.				
12 noon				
1 p.m.				

c Discuss your findings. The following questions should help your discussion.
— How much of your time did you spend on each category listed in the Introduction to this investigation?
— Which category took the largest amount of your time?
— Who has control over more of your set goals?
— Which of your goals could you identify from the way you used your time?
— What values could you identify from the way you used your time?
— Do you use your time more effectively at the weekend or during a school day?
— Did you have any difficulties in allocating your time to the categories suggested above?
— How could you overcome these difficulties?

d Conclusion. What did this investigation tell you about the way you used your time?

Investigation No. 4
Time Management

Introduction

Time is often wasted because we do not think about the job we are about to do. Many tasks we carry out take far longer than necessary, and we waste time and energy that could have been saved. One way of becoming more aware of how we spend time is to carry out a *time and motion study* using a *process chart*.

Aims

● To observe and record the time and motion involved in making up a recipe

- To evaluate the process and to repeat the exercise to see if time and motion can be reduced

Procedure

Note: For this exercise you will need to work with a partner. One person is the worker and one the recorder.

a Choose a quick and simple recipe (for suggested recipes see page 15).

b Draw up a process chart following the example given below (and refer to Appendix, page 193).

Worker	Recorder
— Read the recipe	— Read and check that you understand the process chart (see below)
— Make up the recipe	— Carefully record all processes involved in making up the recipe
— Tidy up the kitchen area	

c Discuss the results of the exercise together. How was time and motion wasted? How could this be improved in a repeat of the exercise? List your approach to repeating the exercise.

d Change places and repeat the exercise.

e Discuss the results again.

Discussion/Conclusion

f Did you take as many steps and processes in the second exercise? How did you go about saving time and movement? What recommendations could you make on time usage from this exercise? What contributed to wasted time and motion?

g What did this exercise teach you? Draw your conclusions.

Process Chart

A process chart is used to find out how time and movement can be saved. There are four different symbols used in the chart:

○ Means that something is being **moved**, for example, a saucepan from the cupboard to the cooker.

◯ Means that an object is being **changed**, for example, chopping parsley or peeling the shell from a hard-boiled egg.

☐ Means that **checking** is occurring, for example, an ingredient is being measured or ingredients simmering in a saucepan are being checked.

▽ Means that there is a **delay** in activity, for example, waiting for fat to heat.

As an activity is occurring, the recorder follows the processes of the worker by drawing a line from one symbol to another and also describing what is happening. For example,

Steps	Movement	Change	Checking	Delay or Storage	Description of Method
	○	○	□	▽	Move knife from drawer
2	○	○	□	▽	Chop parsley
	○	○	□	▽	
	○	○	□	▽	

Recipes to Try

Chicken Noodle Soup

Ingredients

200 ml water
½ teaspoon chopped parsley
1 chicken stock cube
1 tbsp vermicelli or noodles
1 pinch curry powder

Method

1 Combine all ingredients and bring to the boil.
2 Stir once, put lid on saucepan and simmer for 10 mins.

Serves 1

Scotch Egg

Ingredients

100 g sausage meat
1 egg
1 tbsp breadcrumbs
deep frying oil

Method

1 Place egg into a small saucepan and cover with *cold* water.
2 Place on heat and bring to the boil. Time the boiling for 10 mins to hard-boil the egg.
3 Empty hot water from saucepan, crack egg and run cold water over. (This prevents a grey ring forming around the yolk.)
4 Remove shell from egg.
5 Mould sausage meat over egg. Roll in breadcrumbs.
6 Place in hot deep-frying oil for 6–8 mins.

Serves 1.

Frying Rules

- No water in hot oil
- No flames near hot oil
- Lower food into hot oil — don't splash
- Oil gets much hotter than boiling water — take care!

Money

Money is an essential part of our society.
It is a useful resource which enables us
to achieve our goals and to satisfy some of our
needs and wants.

Workshop

1 How much are you worth today?
  a Think about yourself.
  b Try to work out the amount of money that has been spent on you
     recently.
  c Add up the cost of the clothes you are wearing today.
  d Work out the cost of your glasses or contact lenses, your last hair cut.
  e Does the total cost surprise you?
  f Compare it with that of other class members.
  g What is the total cost of the clothing worn by the whole class?

2 How much do you spend?
  Draw up a table in your book like the one below.
  Keep a record for one week of all the money that you actually spend,
include bus fares, school lunches, snacks, leisure activities etc.

Date	Item	Money spent
	Total	

3 What resources are 'free'?
  Is there anything that you have used today that did not cost money?
Discuss.

4 How do you feel about money?
  In your book, complete the following sentences:
  A person who earns £.................. a week is rich.
  When I have no money I feel ....
  When I see something I want to buy I ....
  If someone gave me £25 for my birthday I would ....
  Money is .... important to me.

Investigation No. 5
Income

Aims
- To find out the average income of a group of students
- To find out the source of income
- To find out how the income is spent

Procedure

a All class members are to complete the following survey. Draw up tables like those given below and collate your data.

How much money do you spend each week?

Amount of £	No. of Replies	% of Class
£2 or less		
£5 or less		
£10 or less		
£15 or less		
More than £15		

Where does this money come from?

Source	No. of Replies	% of Class
Regular allowance from parents		
Requested from parents		
From part-time job		
Gift		
Savings		
Other		

How do you spend your money?

Item	No. of Replies	% of Class
Clothes		
Food		
Leisure activities		
Gifts		
School expenses		
Donations to charity		

How frequently do you save money? ....

b Discuss your findings. The following questions will assist you.
— What is the average weekly income of the group?
— Was there a wide variation in the amount of money available to members of the class?
— What was the main source of income for the class?
— What percentage of the class saved regularly?
— Which three items were purchased most often by the majority of students in the class?

c Draw a conclusion from your findings that states what the average income was, what it was used for in the majority of cases, and from where it was obtained.

Purchasing Goods (Spending Money)

Every day of our lives we wear clothes, eat food, use electricity and buy things we want. Any person who uses goods and services is called a **consumer**. Most goods and services we use in our society are paid for with money. **Goods** are material possessions to buy and use, for example, clothing and records. **Services** are actions performed for a consumer, for example, dental work, haircuts and car repairs.

As a consumer you have certain **responsibilities** and **rights**.

Your responsibilities are:
— to be informed;
— to make intelligent choices;
— to follow directions given by manufacturers;
— to make reasonable complaints in relation to poor goods or services (for example, return purchases when they are faulty).

Your rights are:
— to be informed;
— to be heard;
— to receive a safe well-constructed product;
— to expect a product to perform the functions the manufacturer claims it will perform;
— to be able to select between products;
— to receive correct information about product.

It is up to each one of us to use these rights and responsibilities to ensure that we gain value for money.

Advertising (Being enticed to spend money, or being informed)

Advertising is a method used to inform consumers about products. It is important to read advertisements carefully and sift through the information that they contain before you use them as a resource to buy a product.

- Collect three advertisements. Paste each one into your book and beside it comment on its attractiveness, its content, its completeness (that is, how well it describes the product and its function).

- What different methods are used by the advertiser to sell the goods? (For example, attractive people and free gifts.)

- Would you like to buy any of the products? Why?

Where to buy. There are many places from which goods can be purchased.

Can you think of any other places from which goods can be purchased? List the advantages and disadvantages of each of these places at which you spend money.

Planning to shop. Good management involves planning what you want and organising your resources to obtain it. Going shopping without clear goals of your wants or needs can mean that you waste time and money.

- **Case study**

John wants a new portable radio/cassette recorder. He has £120 available to spend. He

19

considers it important that the article has a warranty in case something goes wrong in the first few months. John's mother suggests that John should do some comparison shopping before he buys. (Refer back to page 3 to revise decision making). Assist John with his problem.

a Decide on the brand to buy.

b Check the price at:
— a department store,
— a speciality store (for example, an electrical goods store),
— a market,
— a discount store.

From which store would you decide to buy? Give reasons for your answer.

What influences what you buy? Think about the last item that you bought. What influenced you to buy that particular item?

- With your class, draw up a list of things that may influence the way you spend money, and the goods you purchase.

Compare your list with the one below and discuss any items you failed to include in your list.

Newspaper	Magazine
Noticeboard	Radio
Past experience	Parent
Salesperson	Teacher
Advertisements	Consumer publication
Price tag	Close friend
Labels	Government publication
Television	
Someone's advice	

Personal budgeting (Organising Your Money)

As money is a limited resource for most of us, we cannot always spend it as we wish. Planning how to spend money will assist in reaching goals.

Workshop

1 Plan your expenditure for the next week. Compare your plan with the way you actually spend your money. The plan below will assist you.

Week commencing....................and ending....................		
1 Income		
Pocket money		
Wages		
Gifts		
Totals		
2 Fixed Costs	Planned Expenditure	Actual Expenditure
Lunches		
Fares		
Fees		
Other		
Totals		

3 Flexible Costs	Planned Expenditure	Actual Expenditure
Donations to charity		
Entertainment		
Snacks		
Reading materials		
Gifts		
Chemist		
Clothing		
Totals		

Grand Totals
(add 2 and 3)

2 Compare grand totals with total for 1 (Income).

3 How did your *budget* (plan for spending your money) work?

4 How could you improve your budget?

Family Budgeting (Organising Family Money)

Families have more demands on their money resources than you do as one person. Let us look at how a family can manage money to meet needs and wants.

Case Study

Convinced of the need for a money management plan, the Wilson family has decided to budget its finances for the year. Having kept reasonable records for the past year, the following data is available. The Wilsons have no children.

A Income

Mrs Wilson's Income: Mrs Wilson's monthly take-home pay as an Office Manager is £640. She also lectures at a local college one evening a week on Office Practice. For this she receives monthly take-home pay of, on average, £60 from October to June, inclusive. She also marks examination papers and for this she receives a cheque for £110 in August.
Mr Wilson's Income: Mr Wilson's monthly take-home pay as a Stores Clerk is £580. As well as his basic monthly pay he receives a car allowance of 45p a mile and he generally travels 180 miles a month. Mr Wilson also receives a Christmas bonus equivalent to one month's salary.
Other Income: The Wilsons receive a cheque for approximately £80 in January and July from money they have invested in a building society.

B Expenses

Superannuation: This sum is deducted from Mr and Mrs Wilson's pay and therefore is not counted as an expense in this budget which involves only take-home pay.
Insurance: House insurance is due on 12 February each year and costs £121; house contents insurance is due on 20 January and costs £135. Mr and Mrs Wilson have one car and its insurance costs £186 a year, due 3 March. Mrs Wilson wears contact lenses; the insurance premium is £12 due 18 October. Both Mr and Mrs Wilson have life insurance; the premium for Mr Wilson is £140.16 a year, paid monthly and for Mrs Wilson is £96 a year, paid quarterly starting in March.
Fees: Car tax is £100, due 1 January. Rates on the house are £675 a year but are paid in ten instalments over ten consecutive months starting in January. Water rates are paid quarterly, starting in April, and are £68 a year. Mrs Wilson belongs to a health club with fees of £75 a year, paid in August. Both Mr and

Mrs Wilson are in unions; the subscriptions are paid yearly in April and are £45 for Mr Wilson, £35 for Mrs Wilson.
Debts: The mortgage payments are £256 monthly and repayment of a personal loan (used for house renovation) is £45 a month for the next twelve months.

Savings: The car is paid for but the Wilsons like to put £50 a month aside towards a future car. They have a unit trust savings scheme for £25 a month, and would like to save a further £800 for their annual holiday next August.

Monthly living expenses:

Food	£120
Personal	£120
Petrol	£80
Car maintenance	£25
Entertainment	£80
Clothing	£80
Gas and electricity	£100
Telephone	£30
Home maintenance	£75

Workshop

1 In a table like the one below, list the Wilsons' fixed expenses and flexible expenses.

Fixed Expenses	Cost per month	Flexible expenses	Cost per month
	£ p		£ p

This record can be used by the Wilsons to see how much money *must* be available monthly (fixed) and how much money they would *like* to be available each month (flexible). That is, their needs and wants have been separated.

2 List the months of the year. Beside each month write the Wilson's combined income for that month. Add up their *total* income and divide by 12 to give the average monthly income. This is the amount they work on for their budget.

3 Complete the Wilson family's spending budget and calculate their average monthly expenditure by ruling up the following chart in your book and filling in the details.

4 Draw up graph axes like those on page 24. Use bar charts to plot income and expenditure on a monthly basis—use the data from activities 2 and 3 above.

5 Repeat the above exercise using linear graphs for income and expenditure.

Expense	J	F	M	A	M	J	J	A	S	O	N	D	Annual totals
Insurance													
House													
House contents													
Car													
Contact lenses													
Life insurance (Mr Wilson)													
Life insurance (Mrs Wilson)													
House													
Mortgage													
Rates													
Water rates													
Fuel													
Phone													
Loan													
Maintenance													
Car													
Tax													
'New car' fund													
Maintenance													
Petrol													
Savings													
Unit trusts													
Holiday													
Union subscription													
Mr Wilson													
Mrs Wilson													
Health club													
Personal													
Food													
Entertainment													
Clothing													
Monthly totals													

(Average monthly expenditure = annual expenditure divided by 12)

In activities 3, 4, and 5 you have been shown how to present the *same* data in three different ways.

6 Write a brief report on your findings about the Wilson's budget.

7 If budgeted income does not match budgeted expenses, what should be done about any differences?

8 Is the above budget plan for the Wilsons realistic?

9 From the information given make a list of the assets that the Wilsons have.

10 How highly do the Wilsons value security in the form of saving?

11 Could the Wilsons alter their budget to enable them to save more annually?

12 What credit cards would be available to the Wilsons? When and for what purchases or payments could they be used?

HOW DID YOU EVER GET OVER YOUR ADDICTION TO CREDIT CARDS?

WELL ONE DAY I LOOKED AROUND AT THE THINGS I HAD BOUGHT ON CREDIT AND REALISED THAT I DIDN'T OWN ANY OF THEM. THE BANK OWNED THEM ALL. SO I LET THE BANK HAVE THEM ALL. I WAS SAVED!

ALLELUIA!

Test Yourself

1 What is a consumer?

2 What is money used for in our society?

3 Explain the differences between goods and services.

4 Which of the following statements describe consumer responsibilities? Write the appropriate statements in your book.
— to be heard
— to be informed
— to choose between products
— to make legitimate complaints
— to expect products to be safe
— to follow directions

5 What is a resource?

6 Name resources that are common to most human beings.

7 Discuss what influences the way we use our resources.

8 What is a budget?

9 Define the terms **fixed** and **flexible expenses**.

10 Discuss the possible advantages of managing resources such as time and money.

Food Preparation

Food is considered a basic human need. Many human resources are used in meeting this basic need.

- Make a list of the resources you think are commonly used in meeting the family food needs.
- How many of these resources can be used again?
- Discuss how resources can be saved when meeting family food needs.
  Consider the following ways in which fuel might be wasted while cooking for the family

— Saucepan too small for the hotplate.
— Gas turned up so that it laps up the sides of the saucepan.
— Kettle left boiling long after it has come to the boil.
— Food cooked in saucepan without the lid on, allowing heat to escape.
— Oven door left open longer than needed.

These are a few examples. How many more can you list?

Workshop

1 Role-play ways in which resources are wasted in the family—for example, leaving electrical appliances turned on, using excessive paper products, wasting heat, wasting water or wasting time.

2 a Organise a visit to your class from a representative of British Gas or the electricity authority to discuss more fully with you the ways in which energy can be saved in the home.

b List the ways you learned to save energy in the home from the visiting speaker (ways that you had not listed in 1 above). Tick with a red tick those ways to save energy that your family already puts into action.

3 There are a number of kitchen utensils that have many uses and a number of kitchen utensils that you can manage without by substituting something else (substitution of resources). In your book, complete the following statements to show how resources can be substituted for each other.

a I wished to make a pizza, but I did not have a pizza tray. I used a .... tray — it did not really matter that the pizza was not round.

b My casserole lid is broken, so now when I need a lid I cover it with ....

c I always roll pastry out with a .... because someone borrowed my rolling pin and did not return it.

4 Make up two of your own examples to add to those in activity 3.

5 Consider how you or your family could be less wasteful with food and, therefore, less wasteful with the household money. List two ways this waste could be lessened.

6 a Read the **Case Study** below. List the things that Phillip's mother does to *save* energy and the things that she does that *waste* energy — list these in two separate columns in your book.

Phillip followed his mother around the house on Saturday morning to see how she rated as an energy saver.

- He saw his mother turn off the electric hotplate on the cooker just before the kettle boiled.
- He saw that the saucepan for the eggs was smaller than the hotplate on which it was being used.
- Phillip's mother used the hot water from the tap to start boiling the eggs.
- After breakfast she put on the dishwasher, which was half full. Then it was time to do the laundry.
- Phillip's mother used cold water to wash the clothes and he noticed that all his father's shirts were 'non-iron'.
- When Phillip returned to the kitchen he noticed that mother had left the fan heater turned on although she was upstairs getting dressed.
- Phillip's mother then prepared some vegetables for lunch, washing them in the sink without the plug in position.

b If possible, carry out the above exercises yourself on Saturday or Sunday. Use a parent, brother or sister as a *subject*.

7 Can you help to make decisions that will economise on resources available in your home?

8 Find out the meaning of the word **resourcefulness**.

Investigation No. 6
Resource Economy

Aim

- To become aware of the purpose of being resourceful

Procedure

a Read the recipe at the end of this Practical Investigation. This recipe will be prepared to serve the whole class.

b Discuss how the whole class can economise on the Home Economics Room's resources. For example, is it possible to use only one oven? How many saucepans are really necessary (and, therefore, how many hot-plates)? Is it better to divide up the ingredients for preparation (that is, two people prepare *all* the tomatoes for the whole class, four people prepare *all* the bread rolls, etc.)?

c Draw up a plan to prepare the recipe as many times as needed for everyone.

d Prepare the recipe and serve.

Discussion/Conclusion

— Were there any other means by which the class could have economised? Discuss and write a report on these.

— Why are not all Home Economics practical foods classes conducted like this one, using as few resources as possible? (In other words, what is the *goal* of most Home Economics lessons?)

— Give one example of how the decision making skills you developed in this exercise might help you and your family at home.

Savoury Filled Rolls

Ingredients

4 crusty bread rolls 2–3 days old
25 g margarine
50 g mushrooms
3 small tomatoes
1 small onion
3 eggs
3 shakes pepper

Method

1 Cut a slice from the top of each roll and scoop out most of the soft bread inside.

2 Wash and slice mushrooms.

3 Chop tomatoes.

4 Peel the onion and dice very finely.

5 Melt the margarine, add the vegetables and fry for 5–10 mins until soft but not coloured.

6 Whisk the eggs with the pepper. Pour into the pan

with the vegetables and stir with a wooden spoon over a low heat until the mixture scrambles.

7 Pile the scrambled mixture into the bread rolls, replacing the lids.

8 Place on an oven tray and cook at 200°C, gas mark 6 for about 15 mins until the rolls are crisp and the filling thoroughly heated through.

9 Serve on a small dinner plate accompanied by a glass of water or a glass of milk.

Serves 4.

Money and Food

A considerable proportion of everyone's income is spent on food each week. Because of this, it is important that we obtain good value for money.

- What would you consider to be value for money as far as food is concerned? Make a list.

- Consider the following **Case Study:**

Joanne, Anthony and Maria share a house in Liverpool. Each week they put £30 into a pool to purchase their food. They take it in turns to do the shopping. Joanne returns home from shopping and points out that she overspent the food budget. Anthony and Maria help her unpack the food, and in doing so, notice that she has purchased well-known name brand goods, for example, Findus and John West. Maria points out that they could reduce their costs by using generic (store brand) goods. Joanne says that these products are inferior. An argument between Maria and Joanne develops.

- Discuss: How could you solve their problem? (The workshop at the end of this section will help you.)

What is the real purpose of the label on foods? Is it really only to tell us that a particular packet contains a certain product? If it is, then why do manufacturers go to so much trouble to make the label attractive? Is it a form of advertising? If we are really tempted to buy foods because of a pretty label, what is the role of the 'nameless' cans and packets of food now available which have just a two-toned printed label? How have the manufacturers of these 'nameless' goods maintained sales?

Have a look at a collection of food labels from packets, bags and jars of food. What are some of the basic parts of a label?

The name of the food, the name of the manufacturer, the net weight (that is, the weight of the food without the container) and a list of ingredients are basic to most labels. A few labels provide us with additional information which lists the nutritional value of the food. Two of the most important things on the label, for you the shopper (other than the name of the food) are the list of ingredients and the nutritional value. Get used to reading these and get 'health value' for money by keeping to a minimum those foods with added sugar (sucrose, fructose, dextrose or honey), added salt or large amounts of fat. Try to buy foods which are high in fibre, protein and B complex vitamins particularly riboflavin, thiamin, nicotinic acid, folic acid and B_{12}). In other words, be fussy about what you nourish your body with. Many of us are fussy about how we look on the outside but forget about looking after the mechanics of the body.

Be a food label snoop

Workshop

1 a Examine the labels on a can, a packet and plastic bag of food. Write a brief description of the food from the information supplied on the label.

b Open the containers and examine the contents. Does your description agree with what you see? Taste the contents. Does your description still agree?

Case Study

2 Sian is having a friend over for the afternoon. She enjoys cooking and decides to make a snack for afternoon tea. Sian's mother agrees, but says that if she wants anything other than what is in the kitchen, she has to buy it herself and must finish cooking within an hour. Sian looks in the cupboard and finds flour, milk, sugar, butter, eggs, bread and cheese, tea and coffee. She then looks at her pocket money and finds she has £1.
Solve Sian's afternoon snack problem, by making an afternoon tea for which Sian would not have to spend more than £1 and which is a healthy snack.

3 Purchase a number of labelled food items which can be combined into a healthy meal — that is, one in which the proportions suggested by the Healthy Diet Pyramid (see page 86) are represented. Prepare the meal. The recipes following Investigation No. 7 will help you with your decisions.

Investigation No. 7
Brand Comparisons

Aim

• To compare a number of store brand (generic) and named brand goods.

Procedure

a Select a canned food (for example, tomatoes) available in many different brands.

b Data collection: complete the following table.

Details of Purchase	Store Brand	Named Brand
Contents as stated on can Size of can No. of tomatoes Weight of tomatoes Weight of liquid Colour of tomatoes		

c Make up the tomatoes into a dish (see **Piquant Tomatoes** and **Old Fashioned Tomato and Onion Pie** recipes following this exercise).

---

d Compare the dishes.
— Did the brand used make any noticeable difference to the end result?
— Were there any differences in the flavours?

Discussion/Conclusion
— What recommendations would you make regarding the purchase of tinned tomatoes?
— Which offered the best value for money?

Recipes to Try

Beef, Bean and Bacon Soup

Ingredients

435 g can beef broth
½ can water
425 g can mixed bean salad, drained
3 rashers bacon, fat removed and chopped
½ small onion, finely chopped
1 clove garlic, crushed
parsley for garnish

Method

1 Place all ingredients in a saucepan.

2 Stir and simmer for 5 minutes.

3 Garnish with parsley.

Serves 3

Piquant Tomatoes

Ingredients

15 g margarine
4 spring onions, chopped
400 g can tomatoes, drained
¼ tsp basil
¼ tsp oregano
pepper

Method

1 Melt margarine in a saucepan.

2 Fry spring onions slowly for 2–3 mins.

3 Cut tomatoes in half, add to spring onions together with basil, oregano and pepper.

4 Stir gently, cover pan and simmer for 5 minutes.

5 Serve with meat or chicken or kebabs, or as a sauce with pasta.

Serves 2–3.

Old-fashioned Tomato and Onion Pie

Ingredients

1 medium onion, halved and sliced across
400 g can tomatoes, drained
pepper
50 g margarine
50 g wholemeal breadcrumbs
chopped parsley

Method

1 Grease a shallow ovenproof dish, about 18 cm × 12 cm.

2 Place onions in boiling water and simmer for 3 minutes.

3 Place drained tomatoes in the greased dish.

4 Place onions on top.

5 Melt margarine in a saucepan, remove from heat, stir in breadcrumbs and parsley (if used).

6 Spoon topping evenly over the tomatoes and onions.

7 Bake for 15 minutes in oven at 190°C, gas mark 5.

Serves 2 as main dish, 4 as vegetable dish.

Tuna, Corn and Pepper casserole

Ingredients

1 medium potato (200 g when peeled)
200 ml milk
1 × 185 g can tuna chunks
1 small onion, finely chopped
1 tbsp mayonnaise
ground black pepper
1 × 198 g can sweet corn
½ red pepper, finely chopped
1 tbsp margarine
1 tbsp flour
100 g cheddar cheese, grated
½ tsp paprika

Method

1 Boil the potato and mash with 1 tbsp of the milk. Spread on the bottom of a greased casserole dish about 18 cm diameter.

2 Mix tuna, onion, mayonnaise and black pepper together. Spread over potato.

3 Spread the red pepper and sweet corn evenly over the tuna mixture.

4 Make a white sauce by melting the margarine in a saucepan, adding flour and stirring with a wooden spoon. Cook 1 min (this is called a **roux**). Remove from heat, gradually add milk, stirring constantly. Return to heat, stir until thick.

5 Pour sauce over the corn and pepper, spreading evenly. Top with grated cheese, making sure all the surface is covered.

6 Sprinkle paprika in a line across the cheese. Bake at 180°C, gas mark 4, for 20 minutes.

Serves 4.

Three Bean Salad

Ingredients

50 g canned red kidney beans, drained
50 g canned butter beans, drained
40 g canned chick peas, drained
½ onion, finely chopped
½ clove garlic, crushed
½ green pepper, seeded and finely chopped
1 tbsp chopped parsley
ground black pepper
1½ tbsp vinegar
½ tbsp sunflower oil

Method

1 Mix vinegar and oil.

2 Toss all ingredients together until beans are coated with vinegar and oil.

3 Chill before serving.

4 Serve with grilled beefburgers, fish fingers, cold meat or hard-boiled egg.

Spaghetti Marinara

Ingredients

100 g spaghetti
1 can or jar mussels
2 anchovy fillets
1 × 200 g can tomatoes
½ can prawns
2 tsp chopped parsley
2 tsp oil

Method

1 Cook spaghetti for 10 minutes until just tender (not completely cooked) in a saucepan of boiling water.

2 Chop tomatoes.

3 Cut each anchovy into 3–4 pieces.

4 Heat oil gently in a saucepan, add all drained fish and sauté gently.

5 When spaghetti is tender, drain and add to the tomato. Simmer for 5 minutes.

6 Add all other ingredients and toss lightly.

7 Serve with a side salad of lettuce and cucumber.

Serves 2

3 Resource Savers in the Kitchen

Resource Saver No. 1
The Recipe

DECODING
A RECIPE

Using recipes well will save the resources money, time, energy and food.

What is a Recipe?

It is a list of *ingredients* and the measure of the ingredients required to make a particular dish, as well as a *method* which explains how to prepare the ingredients.

For example:

Creamy Brunch Scramble

Ingredients

2 eggs
1 tb chopped spring onions
1 bread roll/bap
2 slices tomato
1 slice cooked ham
pinch of thyme
25 g margarine
1 tbsp plain low fat yoghurt

Method

1 Beat eggs and thyme. Add onion.
2 Heat 10 g of the margarine in a saucepan, add eggs and yoghurt. Stir over a low heat until the mixture thickens.
3 Split the roll and toast until golden brown, spread with remaining margarine.
4 Place tomato on roll and top with scramble.
5 Cut the slice of ham in half, make it into two rolls and garnish each roll with a ham roll.

Serves 2.

The *name* of a recipe is derived from either the appearance of the dish (for example, Sponge Cake), the flavour of the dish (for example, Sweet and Sour Pork), the historical origin of the dish (for example, Spaghetti Bolognaise from Bologna in Italy), or it could be a combination of reasons such as in the above recipe—a combination of appearance and suitable time to serve.

The amounts of ingredients in a recipe are arrived at by trial and error on the part of the recipe developer. The amounts, or measures, are normally written in an abbreviated form. The abbreviations and amounts used in this book are:

g	=	gram
kg	=	kilogram
ml	=	millilitre
l	=	litre
tbsp	=	level tablespoon
tsp	=	level teaspoon
pinch	=	the amount of an ingredient obtained between two pinched fingers
pkt	=	packet
mins	=	minutes
shake	=	the amount of seasoning or spice obtained by shaking a container, with a sprinkle top, once
drop	=	a drop as it falls from a tilted bottle
1 egg	=	55 g egg (size 4)
1 onion (or other)	=	1 average-sized vegetable

Using the Recipe

Special terms or words are frequently used in recipes. You will find a **glossary** of those used in this book on page 197.

1 **Read** the ingredients carefully.
   Sometimes they are a little tricky and can be misunderstood, for example,
   100 g of rice—this means 100 g of uncooked rice.
   100 g of cooked rice—means 100 g of rice measured *after* it is cooked.
This makes a lot of difference to a recipe as rice trebles in size when cooked.

2 **Measure** ingredients correctly.
   Dry ingredients are measured with scales or a nest of spoons. Dry ingredients should be filled into a spoon so that the measure is full (no air pockets). Dry ingredients should not be *pressed* into measures firmly unless the recipe asks for 1 firmly packed spoon of ......
   Liquid is measured in a graduated jug and should be read with the graduated jug on a level surface and your eye level with measuring line in question.

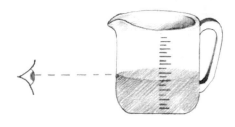

   Spoon measures given in a recipe are *level* measures. The spoon should be slightly over-filled, then levelled with a spatula.

Ingredients shaken or pressed to level do not give an accurate measure.

3 **Interpret the recipe.**

There should not be any need to alter the amounts of ingredients listed in a recipe. A recipe used for the first time should be followed exactly. When you use the recipe again and you wish to add or subtract any ingredient, discuss it with your teacher first. It is easy to unbalance a well worked-out recipe just as it is easy to add or subtract *some* ingredients. It is not only wasteful of ingredients to alter some recipes, but it can produce disappointing results.

It is important that the method of a recipe is followed as written if the recipe developer's intended result is to be produced. With some recipes it is possible to alter the method with little or no influence on the finished result. Always discuss this with your teacher because, as with changes to quantities, you might waste the ingredients by producing an undesirable product. To experiment with this, work your way through Investigation No. 8, The Cake Mix.

One very important point to note in regard to the method is that *any cooking time suggested* — for example, 'Stir for 2 mins until the mixture thickens', or 'bake at 180°C for 20 mins' — *is only a guide*. It is impossible to give absolutely accurate cooking times for dishes which will be cooked in a great variety of ovens or on gas jets or electric hot plates. Some guidance is usually needed at first until the cook understands how to tell when a particular dish is cooked; how to know when the meat is 'seared' or when it is 'browned', and what is meant by 'cook until thick enough to coat the spoon'. These are areas in which you will learn, by watching and listening to your teacher, to develop sufficient skills and knowledge to manage alone.

Workshop

1 Prepare a recipe from those on pages 40–41. Prepare a list, similar to the one below, and see how you rate as your teacher checks your work.

Management Exercise Check-list	*Yes*	*No*
a Reads the recipe right through before beginning preparation.	___	___
b Collects all ingredients and equipment before beginning preparation.	___	___
c Measures ingredients correctly.	___	___
d Follows each step of the method carefully.	___	___
e Serves food in an appealing manner.	___	___
f Uses desired safety measures while working in the Home Economics Room.	___	___

g Puts away all unused ingredients and cleans   _____   _____
   equipment when finished.
h Completes the preparation of the recipe and   _____   _____
   cleans up in time allowed.

2 Prepare the **Creamy Brunch Scramble** recipe on page 33 but
   halve the ingredients so that you are making it for 1 only.

3 The following recipe case studies are presented for you to understand
   managing a recipe for a particular occasion.

Case Study A

Mrs Jones is having ten people for a meal on Saturday evening. She has
found the following recipe in a magazine and would like to make it.

Fragrant Country Chicken

Ingredients

2 tbsp oil
1 large onion, sliced
3 rashers bacon, diced
150 g sliced celery
397 g can whole tomatoes
finely grated rind of 1 orange
juice of 1 orange
1 sliced orange
2 tsp cornflour
1 tbsp water
sugar, salt and pepper to taste
1 cooked chicken

Method

1 Remove chicken flesh from bones and cut into
   bite-sized pieces.

2 Heat oil in a large saucepan and add onion and
   bacon. Cook gently until onion is transparent, add
   celery, can of tomatoes, orange rind and juice. Boil
   mixture, reduce heat, cover and simmer for 5 mins.

3 Blend cornflour with water and stir into tomato
   mixture with a little sugar, salt and pepper. Simmer
   a further 3 mins.

4 Add chicken to sauce and heat through.

5 Garnish with orange slices.

Serves 5.

Mrs Jones notices that the recipe is for five people. Can you change the
recipe so it will be enough for ten people?

a Rewrite the ingredients on a separate piece of paper with amounts
   suitable for ten people.

b Draw up a shopping list for Mrs Jones making sure you put all of the
   same type of foods together to make the shopping easier.

b Mrs Jones is not sure of the meanings of the following terms in the
   recipe: **transparent, rind, rasher, simmer, garnish.**
Can you help her? Write the meanings in your book.

Case Study B

Caroline lives in a flat by herself. Tomorrow evening she has invited a
friend for a meal. The **Lemon Lamb Casserole** recipe below is what
she has chosen to serve.

Lemon Lamb Casserole

Ingredients

25 g margarine
4 lamb chops
1 sliced onion
1 clove of garlic, crushed
375 ml water

1 tsp finely grated lemon rind
75 ml lemon juice
1 chicken stock cube
¼ tsp thyme
50 g sultanas
3 shakes pepper
4 medium sized potatoes
3 courgettes, sliced

Method

1 Heat margarine in pan. Sauté chops until brown. Place them into a casserole dish.
2 Cook onion and garlic in pan until slightly brown, add water, lemon rind and juice, stock cube, thyme, sultanas, pepper, and bring to the boil.
3 Peel potatoes, cut into large dice and place on chops.

4 Top with lemon mixture, cover and bake at 180°C, gas mark 4 for 1 hour.
5 Add courgettes, cover and bake a further 15 mins or until meat is tender.

a Rewrite the amounts of the ingredients Caroline will need for her meal.

b Caroline needs to know what is meant by **sauté** and **dice**. Write the meanings out for her.

c Caroline wants to prepare as much of the dish as she can tonight and reheat it tomorrow night. Suggest to what stage she could prepare the recipe tonight.

4 The following cookery terms can be found in the word search on page 38. The words read vertically, horizontally and diagonally as well as forwards or backwards. Circle the words as you find them. One has been done to guide you.

Words

bake	fillet	peel	skim
baste	fry	pickle	skin
batter	glaze	poach	steam
beat	grate	roast	stew
blend	grease	sauté	stone
boil	grill	season	strain
braise	mash	sieve	stuff
casserole	mince	simmer	toast
drain	parboil	slice	whisk

Puzzle

```
U T S A O T K L E E P N X H E L K C I P
P H N I A R D V S T Z W J C S D M M I Q
S F I B T Z U A C E E A Y C S A B A I Y
E L I O B E K U F H S L L S T N M E E A
A I G R E A S E K C P I L G U I S T E W
S N P Y Z K U W Y S V C A I F T S S V W
O C R X E W F D T I A K D R F A D R R D
N F E R C I T O E S K N L C B E M W W S
G G U K N W N S S C E E J K T G R R O L
W R O H I E T E G L I E E U G Q H Y I Q
R M I E M R R R B R K L A H T I W O G H
Z J A L A O S G E A A S S E T B T O W
S Z M I L Y S H B T G T A T F R A O U K
I R N E C N I N O Z T O E H A S N E S B
E H T A Q G M M O Q R A C P K I N I B I
V C H H W V M H E H M A B I K W H M B G
E V F Z D P E L G Y O Y M S U W Q E V M
T P H C S C R Z V P J E K C V H P C R I
```

Questions

a Define all the items that begin with B (see **Glossary** on page 197).
b Find *one* recipe that uses *four* of the terms in the puzzle.
c Explain the difference between:
   — boil and simmer
   — toast and grill
   — whisk and beat
   — roast and bake
   — skin and peel
   — braise and stew.

Investigation No. 8
The Cake Mix

Aim
● To discover how changing the ingredients and the method of a recipe influences the product

Procedure
a You will require one identical plain packet cake mix each (bulk mix can be purchased from flour wholesalers).

b Each member of the class is to proceed to prepare his/her mix with different instructions, as follows. (Lesson cost can be reduced by pupils working in groups and/or fewer procedures being undertaken.)

Pupil No.	Procedure for preparation of cake mix
1	Prepare as per instructions on the packet.
2	Prepare as per instructions on the packet but with milk instead of water for the liquid.
3	Prepare as per instructions on pack but with orange juice instead of water for the liquid.
4	Prepare by adding water first then egg.
5	Prepare by adding milk first then egg.
6	Use 2 eggs and only ½ the liquid as per instructions on the packet.
7	Use 125 g melted butter to bind packet ingredients and press into slab tin.
8	Use 100 g melted butter and 1 egg and shape into biscuits.
9	Make up as per packet and leave in oven 10 mins beyond recommended cooking time.
10	Make up as per pack and take out of oven 10 mins before recommended cooking time.
11	Make up as per instructions on the packet and cook in an electric oven at oven temperature 20°C higher than recommended.
12	Make up as per instructions on the packet and cook in a gas oven at oven temperature one gas mark higher than recommended.
13	Make up as per instructions on the packet and cook in an electric oven at oven temperature 20°C lower than recommended.
14	Make up as per instructions on the packet and cook in gas oven at oven temperature one gas mark lower than recommended.
15	Use 50 ml less water and add 100 g mixed fruit.
16	Use cold coffee as liquid.
17	Mix egg and liquid together first then gradually add cake mix.
18	Use 125 g melted butter and 100 g mixed fruit or nuts and cook in slab tin.
19	Use 2 eggs and half the liquid. Separate whites and yolks of eggs. Mix yolks and liquid into mix. Beat whites, fold in.
20	Use 4 eggs only as the liquid, add all at once.

(Each pupil needs a copy of these procedures.)

c Write on a square of paper your pupil number and how your cake was handled. When all are prepared place them all together where the class can see. Label with your paper square.

d Examine all the finished results. Each will need to be cut so texture can be examined. Taste as many as possible. Draw up an observation table like the one on the following page to record and score your results. (A sample is completed to guide you.)

Sample	Rating of Results									Total Score
	9 Ex.	8 V.G.	7 G.	6 Sat.	5 Av.	4 Fair	3 Poor	2 V. Poor	1 Unacceptable	
Sample No. 1										
Appearance		8								
Texture				6						21
Taste			7							
Sample No. 2										
Appearance										
Texture										
Taste										

e Total the scores from the whole class.

Discussion/Conclusion
— Which samples rated the highest?
— Which methods will you use again? Why?
— What variables were there in this exercise other than the different methods? (This refers to human resources, non-human resources, etc.)
— How might these have influenced the results?

Recipes to Try

Drop Scones

Ingredients
150 g S.R. flour
1 egg
½ tsp oil
150 ml milk

Method

1 Sift flour into a bowl.

2 Make a well in the flour and break egg in whole. Mix in ever-increasing circles, gradually taking in some of the flour.

3 When egg is mixed to a paste, gradually add milk into well and continue mixing as before until all flour is taken up.

4 Beat briskly with a wooden spoon to make a smooth batter.

5 Heat a wide flat pan or electric frying pan, grease with about ½ tsp oil.

6 Drop batter from a dessertspoon onto the hot pan, so that the scones will be round.

7 Allow to cook until bubbles are appearing on top of the batter. When first bubble bursts, turn the scone carefully with a spatula or palate knife. If any batter sticks to the spatula remove it immediately or it will cause you to tear your scones when you turn them.

8 Cook on the other side for 1–2 mins until golden brown. *Do not* press the scone down when you turn it, this expels the air bubbles and makes the scones rubbery.

9 Place in a clean tea towel until they are cool.

Makes about 12 scones.

Honey Oat Bars

Ingredients

100 g rolled oats
150 g sultanas
75 g wholemeal S.R. flour
50 g raw sugar
50 g coconut
150 g margarine
1 tbsp honey

Method

1 Combine oats, sultanas, sifted flour (return husks from sifter to basin), sugar and coconut in a basin.

2 Melt the margarine and honey together in a saucepan.

3 Mix the melted ingredients into the dry ingredients until the mixture clings together. Press evenly over the base of a well-greased 28 cm × 18 cm tin. Bake at 180°C, gas mark 4 for 15–20 mins or until golden.

4 Cut into bars.

Bran Biscuits

Ingredients

75 g wholemeal plain flour
2 tsp baking powder
1 tsp raw sugar
50 g unprocessed bran

60 g margarine
2 tbsp water
25 g unprocessed bran, extra

Method

1 Sift flour and baking powder into basin, return husks from sifter to basin.

2 Add sugar and bran. Rub in margarine.

3 Add enough of the water to bind ingredients together. Turn on to a *lightly* floured (wholemeal) surface, knead until smooth.

4 Sprinkle top with extra bran.

5 Roll to wafer thinness, cut into 5 cm rounds with a cutter.

6 Place on lightly greased oven trays.

7 Bake at 180°C, gas mark 4 for 10–15 mins.

8 Cool on trays.

Makes about 20.

Use as for dry biscuits.

Resource Saver No. 2
The Oven

To manage successfully and economically in the kitchen, it is important for you to understand your oven.

Investigation No. 9
Oven Management

Aim

- To discover the ways in which heat is distributed in a gas oven and an electric oven.

Procedure

a Organise a gas oven and an electric oven (not a fan oven) so that they have *three* shelves—one placed on the top rung, one in the middle and one on the bottom rung.

b Light the ovens simultaneously and set on 220°C or gas mark 7.

c Quickly organise 6 groups in the class to produce a batch of **scones**

each (see recipe on page 44), all cut with the same size cutter and all 2 cm in thickness (that is, you need 6 batches of identical scones).

d *Simultaneously* place all six trays of scones into the two ovens on the previously arranged shelves.

Note: When putting a tray in an oven, it should be placed as it best 'fits' the oven. In most cases, this means that the *long* sides of a rectangular tray should be parallel to the oven door. For example:

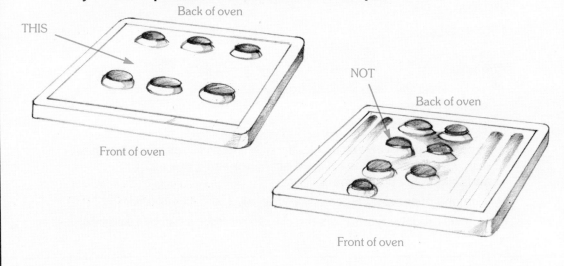

e After 15 minutes remove *all* trays from ovens and record results in a table like the one below.

Tray identification	Scone colour on top	Scone colour on bottom	Tick one column		
			Overcooked	Cooked	Uncooked
Top shelf gas Mid shelf gas Bottom shelf gas Top shelf electric Mid shelf electric Bottom shelf electric					

f Any scones identified as uncooked can be placed back on the original shelf to complete the cooking process — record the time.

g As each tray is cooked and removed from the oven, record the extra time involved and the browning on the top and the bottom of the scone.

h Taste a scone (or half a scone) from each tray and record your results by *ticking* columns in a table like the one below.

Tray identification	Burnt top	Burnt bottom	Too crisp	Tough	Light and tasty	Unacceptable	Acceptable
Top shelf gas Mid shelf gas Bottom shelf gas Top shelf electric Mid shelf electric Bottom shelf electric							

Conclusions

Answer the following questions:
— What differences did you notice between the two ovens as far as heat distribution was concerned?
— Which oven was quickest to produce cooked scones?
— How could you utilise the obvious zones of heat in the gas oven when preparing a meal?

Note: If time does not permit to make scones place a sheet of white paper on each of six trays and make observations relating to colouring of the paper.

Add grated cheese

Extra Notes About Oven Management

Electric ovens take slightly longer to heat up and cool down than gas because of extra insulation in the electric cooker.

As no by-products are formed when using electricity the ventilation provided is small because it is only required to draw off steam from the cooking.

Gas cookers require a larger area of ventilation, the flue, because as gas and air are burned to provide heat, various by-products are formed. Steam is also produced in cooking. Both by-products and steam are removed through the flue.

The following table shows the temperatures that correspond to the terms used in recipes to indicate the heat of the oven.

Oven Temperatures

Electric °C	Gas mark
140°C	1 cool
150°C	2 cool
160°C	3 moderate
180°C	4 moderate
190°C	5 fairly hot
200°C	6 fairly hot
220°C	7 hot
230°C	8 very hot

- Prepare one of the recipes that follow the **Scone** recipe to demonstrate your understanding of oven management.

Recipes to Try

Scones

Ingredients

100 g S.R. flour
100 g wholemeal S.R. flour
50 g margarine
125 ml milk
pinch of salt

Method

1 Sift flours and salt together into a bowl, return husks to bowl.

2 Rub the margarine into the flour until the mixture resembles breadcrumbs.

3 Make a well in the flour and add all the milk at once. Mix to a soft dough.

4 Turn on to a *lightly* floured board and knead *gently* for 30 seconds (too much kneading makes tough scones).

5 Roll or pat the mixture to 2 cm in thickness and cut into shapes. Glaze with a little milk.

6 Bake on a clean dry tray at 220°C, gas mark 7 for 12–15 mins.

Makes 12 scones.

Sultana Carrot Cake

Ingredients

225 g wholemeal plain flour.
1 tsp bicarbonate of soda
½ tsp mixed spice
½ tsp cinnamon
175 g sultanas
125 g grated carrots
2 eggs
175 ml sunflower or maize oil
100 g sugar

Method

1 Sift together flour, bicarbonate of soda, spice and cinnamon (return to bowl any husks left in sifter), mix in the sultanas, carrots and sugar, make a well in centre.

2 With a fork, beat together eggs and oil, add to the bowl, stir in mixture from around the sides of the bowl and then beat well.

3 Turn into a well-greased 18 cm cake tin and bake in a 180°C, gas mark 4, oven for about 60 mins, or until done when tested. Leave in tin for 5 mins and then carefully turn out on to a cooling rack.

Poppy Seed Plait

Ingredients

15 g fresh yeast (or 1 envelope dried yeast)
1 tsp raw sugar
125 ml lukewarm milk
¼ tsp salt
250 g wholemeal flour
25 g margarine
1 tbsp poppy seeds
egg glaze (*Note:* To be mixed for whole class.)

Method

1 Crumble yeast into small bowl or cup, add half the warm milk and the sugar. Stir a little. Leave to stand in a warm place until the mixture becomes frothy (about 15 mins).

2 If using dried yeast follow the instructions on the packet.

3 Sift salt and flour, add husks back into flour.

4 Rub margarine into the flour.

5 Add the yeast mixture and sufficient of the remaining milk to make elastic dough.

6 Knead the dough for 10 mins—the kneading is important to stretch the gluten in the flour.

7 Divide the mixture into 3 equal portions and roll each into a sausage shape about 25 cm long.

8 Press the 3 ends together and plait the bread, tucking the ends under for neatness. Place on a greased tray.

9 Brush neatly and thoroughly with egg glaze and sprinkle with poppy seeds (sesame seeds can be used as an alternative). Cover and leave in a warm (*not hot*) place until the mixture has doubled its size (about 25 mins).

10 Bake at 220°C, gas mark 7 for 20 mins.

Resource Saver No. 3
The Microwave Oven

The Action of a Microwave Oven

Microwaves make the water molecules in food vibrate. (A molecule is a very tiny part of a substance.) They vibrate so rapidly that they cause heat. This heat cooks the food as it is conducted throughout the food. When an ordinary oven cooks food, the heat starts on the outside of the food and gradually moves inwards.

Heat in an Ordinary Oven

The molecules heat up layer by layer. The first layer of heated molecules pass (conduct) their heat on to the next layer, this layer to the next and so on. We, therefore get a brown, crisp outer layer and and a soft inner layer.

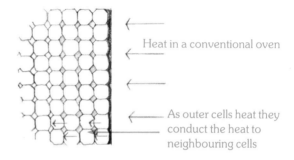

Heat in a conventional oven

As outer cells heat they conduct the heat to neighbouring cells

Heat in a Microwave Oven

Microwaves penetrate the food causing water molecules to vibrate. The vibration causes heat which is conducted to the molecules either side—so speeding the cooking process.

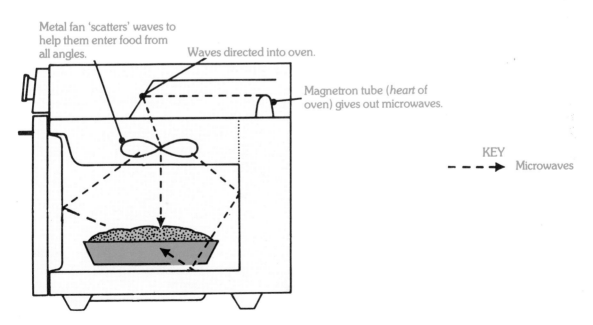

Metal fan 'scatters' waves to help them enter food from all angles.

Waves directed into oven.

Magnetron tube (*heart* of oven) gives out microwaves.

KEY
- - - → Microwaves

45

The depth of penetration of microwaves varies but is only ever 7–9 cm.

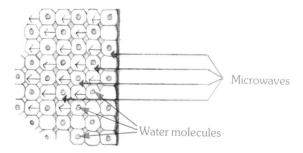

Microwaves

Water molecules

As a result of the method of cooking, there is no browning and no crisping in a microwave oven and the food is cooked quickly. In the microwave oven the waves are given out by a **magnetron** tube. This is the most expensive part of the oven. There are many different types of microwave ovens available. At the moment, these are being up-dated constantly, so it is advisable to read thoroughly the instruction booklet that comes with an oven. When a microwave oven is working the microwaves from the magnetron are directed into the oven where a metal stirrer fan rotates and scatters the waves throughout the oven as they hit the blades of the fan.

The scattered waves are deflected when they hit the metal walls of the oven (see diagram on page 45). This scattering of the waves helps the cooking to be even; that is, the waves enter the food from all angles, not just directly from the magnetron. You must not use metal containers in the oven because the waves are reflected off metal. Metal in the microwave oven produces a risk of the waves going back into the magnetron (called arcing),

damaging the magnetron and causing very expensive repairs. Even the use of a silver or gold pattern on a plate is unwise. Plastic, glass and china can be used, but take care that they are microwave-proof because, although the waves go right through them (they contain no water), the hot food may cause them to crack or melt. You can buy special microwave cookware if you wish.

Uses of Microwave Ovens

- **Reheating cooked foods:** Very good for most foods but not pastry (remember there is no crisping).

- **Thawing frozen food:** Saves you having to remember to take it from the freezer the day before. Do not forget, however, that the waves penetrate no more than 7–9 cm so there is need to allow some time for the heat to be conducted to other areas.

- **Cooking food:** The size of the food, the amount put into the oven, as well as how close the water molecules are together all influence the length of time needed to cook food. Most foods can be cooked in microwave ovens but the food will not brown unless the oven has a special browner or browning dish. The oven needs no preheating. If the oven does not have a turntable, it is a good idea to open the oven and stir or rearrange the food at least once during cooking, to be sure of even cooking. There are now combined microwave and convection ovens available which enable all cooking to be successful. Convection ovens are described later.

Workshop

1 Prepare two separate quantities of one of recipes at the end of this workshop. Cook one quantity in the microwave oven and one in a conventional gas or electric oven. Record the cooking time for each quantity. When both quantities are cooked, compare the two and rate

for appearance, odour and flavour. Draw up a tables in your book similar to the one below and record your ratings by ticking the appropriate boxes.

Appearance

	Very Good	Good	Satisfactory	Fair	Poor
Microwave Oven					
Conventional Oven					

(Draw up similar tables for texture and flavour.)

2 Find out how much it costs to run a microwave oven per minute. Discover the same data for a conventional electric oven and a conventional gas oven. Calculate the cost of power used for both types of oven in activity 1 above.

Microwave Oven Recipes to Try

Liver & Tomato Casserole

Ingredients

250 g lambs or pigs liver
1 large onion, finely chopped
1 tbsp flour
2 rashers lean bacon
397 g can tomatoes
salt and pepper
¼ tsp mixed herbs

Method

1 Wash liver in cold salted water.

2 Trim slices and remove blood vessels.

3 Toss in seasoned flour to which the herbs have been added.

4 Place in casserole dish together with the chopped onion.

5 Remove rind from the bacon and lay the rashers on top of the liver.

6 Add the tomatoes and juice.

7 Cover loosely with cling film.

8 Heat on full power for about 13 minutes.

Serves 4

Stuffed Green Peppers

Ingredients

4 medium green peppers, washed
600 g minced steak
100 g uncooked rice
1 small onion, finely chopped
¼ tsp dried oregano leaves
⅛ tsp garlic powder
80 ml water, milk or tomato juice
1 egg, slightly beaten
2 tbsp tomato paste
50 g grated tasty cheese

Method

1 Cut green peppers in half lengthwise, remove core and seeds.

2 Place peppers, hollow side up, in a shallow, heat-resistant baking dish.

3 In a medium bowl, combine beef, rice, onion, pepper, oregano, garlic powder, water, egg and tomato paste. Mix until thoroughly combined.

4 Spoon mixture into pepper halves.

5 Sprinkle tasty cheese over peppers.

6 Heat, covered loosely with plastic film, full power for 19–22 mins or until meat is cooked and peppers are as tender as desired.

7 Allow to stand 4 mins, covered, before serving.

Serves 4.

Easy Rissoles

Ingredients

100 g minced cooked meat
100 g soft wholemeal breadcrumbs
1 small onion, minced
1 tbsp finely chopped green pepper
1 tbsp chopped parsley
salt and pepper
1 egg, beaten
seasoned flour
1 tbsp oil

Method

1 Combine meat, breadcrumbs, onion, green pepper, parsley, salt and pepper with beaten egg.

2 Divide mixture into six portions and shape into rissoles. Coat with seasoned flour.

3 Preheat browning dish on full power for 5 mins, add oil.

4 Place rissoles into browning dish and cook on full power for 2 mins each side.

Serves 6.

Fresh Cauliflower au Gratin

Ingredients

½ medium cauliflower
2 tbsp water
25 g flour
125 ml milk
25 g margarine
50 g grated tasty cheese
paprika

Method

1 Wash cauliflower and separate into florets.

2 Place florets and water into a deep casserole dish.

3 Heat, covered, on full power for 8–9 mins. Set aside.

4 In a medium-sized bowl melt margarine, uncovered, on full power for 30 seconds.

5 Blend in flour, stir until smooth. Gradually add milk.

6 Heat, uncovered, on full power for 1–2 mins or until sauce is thickened and smooth. Stir once.

7 Stir cheese into sauce.

8 Pour sauce over cauliflower and heat, uncovered on full power for 1–2 mins or until cauliflower is heated through.

9 Sprinkle paprika over sauce before serving.

Serves 4.

Note: Whole cauliflower gives excellent results when cooked on full power. If time allows, cook fresh cauliflower on full power for 12–15 mins.

Fruit Slice

Ingredients

125 g margarine
1 egg, beaten
1 tsp vanilla essence
50 g coconut
150 g S.R. flour, sifted
200 g mixed fruit
150 g brown sugar
cinnamon

Method

1 Mix brown sugar with melted margarine and add egg.

2 Add vanilla and all other ingredients.

3 Press into a greased oblong 26 cm × 16 cm pyrex dish.

4 Dust with cinnamon, cook on full power for 7 mins.

5 Allow to stand 5 mins and cut into squares.

6 Cool in the dish.

Resource Saver No. 4 The Pressure Cooker

Food can be cooked in pressure cookers in steam produced from liquid under high pressure. Food is placed in a cooker, the lid is clamped on and then it is heated until steam issues from the vent pipe in a firm steady stream. The weight is then placed on the vent. This weight 'jiggles' on the pipe to release small amounts of the steam under pressure — there should be a continual hiss of steam.

The cooking time commences when the weight is placed in position. Some other types of cookers have a dial indicating pressure and do not lose steam from under the weight. This type of pressure cooker requires less water than the 'jiggle weight' type.

The pressure inside the cooker increases to 15 lbs per square inch, which causes water to boil at 121°C instead of 100°C. Cooking time is therefore reduced to about a quarter of the normal time. For example, a stew needs 30 minutes cooking time instead of 2 hours or more. The increase in temperature is achieved because steam is retained in the cooker and not allowed to evaporate. Nutritional value of food is retained as fewer nutrients are lost during cooking than by any other method of cooking. Following the initial purchasing cost of the cooker, there is very little maintenance. Only the normal washing and very occasional

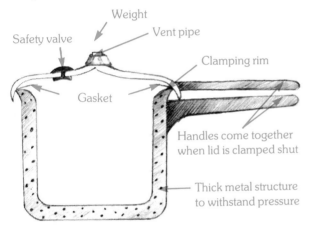

replacement of the gasket are required. The time and fuel savings are considerable and with meat cookery there is very little shrinkage of the meat.

The pressure must be lowered *inside* the cooker before opening, either by allowing it to stand off the hob for 15 minutes before opening or by putting the cooker in the sink and running cold water on the lid until there is no hissing sound left. Ask your teacher to demonstrate this for you. Opening the lid without pressure reduction can cause the boiling contents to be ejected upwards.

Pressure Cooker Recipes to Try
Leek and Potato Soup
Ingredients

2 leeks (white part only)
250 g peeled, quartered potatoes
1 tbsp oil
1 chicken stock cube
500 ml water
pepper

Method

1 Slice the leeks; heat the oil in the bottom of the pressure cooker and fry the leeks until golden brown.

2 Add the potatoes, crumbled stock cube, pepper and water; bring up to pressure and pressure cook at 15 lbs pressure for 8 minutes. Then reduce pressure to room temperature.

3 Liquidise the soup, return to the pan and bring to the boil.

4 Serve garnished with chopped parsley and accompanied by croutons, or crisp bread rolls.

Goulash
Ingredients

500 g stewing steak
1 tbsp seasoned flour
2 onions
1 tbsp oil
1 crushed clove of garlic (optional)
1 small can of tomatoes
1 beef stock cube
250 ml water
1–2 tbsp paprika pepper
350 g small potatoes
75 ml natural yoghurt
1 tbsp chopped parsley

Method

1 Cut meat into 25 mm cubes and toss in seasoned flour.

2 Slice the onions.

3 Heat the oil in the bottom of the pressure cooker and fry the onions and meat until lightly brown; stir in the crushed garlic and paprika pepper.

4 Add the tomatoes, crumbled stock cube and the water; bring to the boil and pressure cook at 15 lbs pressure for 16 minutes.

5 Reduce the pressure and remove the lid, add the potatoes and stir well; if necessary add a little more water.

6 Pressure cook for a further 4 minutes.

7 Add the yoghurt and serve in casserole, garnished with chopped parsley.

Serves 4.

Resource Saver No. 5 Roasting Bags

The concept of wrapping food before cooking has existed almost since the cooking of food became commonplace. Food has been wrapped in leaves, clay, paper and, of course, foil.

Roasting bags have existed now for over ten years. They are transparent bags made from a polyester film which is very strong and will withstand temperatures of up to 200°C.

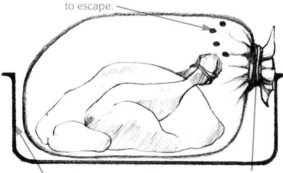

Pierce 3–4 holes in bag near tie end for steam to escape.

Containing dish should be large enough so bag does not hang over sides. It should be no more than 5 cm deep.

Tie securely (use string in microwave oven).

Roasting bags can be used in conventional and microwave ovens. In a microwave oven tie the bag with string *not* the metal thread tie provided with the bag.

Roasting Bags:

• save both cooking time and washing up time;

• retain the nutritional value of food providing juices are served;

• enable cheaper cuts of meat to be kept moist and tenderised;

• enable food, such as casserole dishes, to be prepared in the bag, frozen in the bag and then cooked when required;

• are easy for making up dishes from leftovers;

• reduce the shrinkage of food during cooking, especially meat.

Roasting Bag Recipes to Try

(Remember, if using roasting bags in a microwave oven, tie with *string*)

Sausage and Tomato Casserole

Ingredients

250 g sausagemeat
1 large onion, finely chopped
397 g can of tomatoes
pinch dried basil
pinch salt and pepper

Method

1 Divide sausagemeat into 8 even sized pieces.

2 Roll in seasoned flour.

3 Arrange roasting bag in shallow baking dish.

4 Place in a roasting bag together with the chopped onions.

5 Pour the tomatoes and juice over the balls.

6 Sprinkle on the basil.

7 Tie the bag and make holes in the top of the bag.

8 Bake at 190°C, gas mark 5 for 30 minutes or for 16 minutes in a microwave on full power.

Serves 4

Stuffed Cabbage Rolls

Ingredients

3 large cabbage leaves
250 g minced beef
½ tsp pepper
1 medium onion
1 tbsp tomato ketchup
1 tsp Worcestershire sauce
½ egg, lightly beaten
1 tsp flour
125 ml red wine vinegar
½ can tomato soup
pinch sugar
1 roasting bag

Method

1 Partly cook cabbage leaves in boiling water.

2 Arrange oven bag in a shallow baking dish.

3 Combine mince, seasoning, onion, sauces and egg.

4 Remove coarse centre vein from cabbage leaves and cut each leaf in two. Divide meat mixture into 6 equal portions, roll each in flour and place on cabbage leaf.

5 Roll each leaf up as a parcel, secure with cocktail sticks if necessary, and place in roasting bag.

6 Combine soup, vinegar and sugar; pour over rolls. Tie bag and make holes in top of bag. Bake at 180°C, gas mark 4 for 45 mins or for 16 mins in a microwave on full power.

Serves 3.

Waterfront Pie (using leftovers)

Ingredients

250 ml white sauce
200 g cooked fish
150 g cooked mixed vegetables
½ tsp dried dill
white pepper
2 cooked potatoes
1 tsp margarine
pinch chilli powder
1 roasting bag
1 tbsp flour

Method

1 Place flour in oven bag and shake until evenly covered.

2 Arrange bag in a shallow baking dish.

3 Flake fish and combine with vegetables, dill, and pepper to taste, fold fish into sauce.

4 Spread mixture over base of bag, layer potatoes over fish.

5 Level with fork and dot with small pieces of margarine.

6 Lightly sprinkle potatoes with chilli. Tie bag, make 3 or 4 holes in top near tie end. Bake at 180°C, gas mark 4 for 25 mins or until fish is hot and top is golden.

Serves 4.

Minted Carrots

Ingredients

500 g young carrots
50 g margarine, cut into pieces
black pepper
2 tsp finely chopped fresh mint
1 roasting bag with 1 tbsp flour shaken evenly in bag

Method

1 Arrange floured oven bag in shallow baking dish.

2 Place all ingredients into bag. Tie bag. Make 3 or 4 holes in top of bag at tie end. Bake at 180°C for 20 mins or in a microwave on full power for 3 mins.

Serves 4.

Brown Betty Flake

Ingredients

50 g cornflakes
50 g melted margarine
75 g brown sugar
500 g plums or peaches, stoned and quartered
1 roasting bag

Method

1 Arrange oven bag in shallow 20 cm round baking dish.

2 Gently combine cornflakes with margarine and 50 g sugar. Spread half cornflake mixture over base of bag.

3 Layer fruit into bag. Sprinkle with remaining sugar.

4 Spread remaining cornflakes over fruit. Tie bag. Make 3 or 4 holes in top of bag at tie end. Bake in moderate oven (180°C, gas mark 4) for 30 mins or in a microwave on full power for 8 mins.

Serves 4.

Citrus Nut Chicken

Ingredients

1.5 kg chicken, quartered or 4-chicken pieces
2 tbsp plain flour
375 ml fresh orange juice
¼ tsp pepper
25 g margarine
¼ tsp cinnamon
¼ tsp ground ginger
50 g flaked almonds
75 g raisins
1 orange, cut into segments
1 roasting bag

Method

1 Arrange oven bag in shallow baking dish.

2 Place chicken quarters into bag.

3 Combine flour and orange juice. Add remaining ingredients.

4 Pour mixture over chicken. Tie bag. Make 3 or 4 holes in top of bag at tie end. Bake at 180°C, gas mark 4 for 1 hour or in microwave on full power for 23 mins.

Serves 4.

Resource Saver No. 6
The Convection Oven

The convection oven has been used by professional chefs for many years. Now the convection cooking principle of fan-circulated hot air has been adapted for home use. You can purchase convection ovens as

- work-top equipment
- a built-in unit;
- a free standing cooker

A convection oven is really a conventional oven with a fan. It heats the food much faster than the motionless air of the conventional oven because the hot air of the oven is moving. Just think: which is the quicker way to dry your hair? Sitting in front of the heater or using a hair dryer that blows hot air? Cooking time is reduced for some recipes and the cooking temperature is lowered for nearly all recipes. No special bake-ware is required and the oven shelves can be filled to capacity, allowing just a little air-space between containers and between the containers and the oven walls. This is one of the great advantages of this oven over the microwave because the more food you put in a microwave the greater the cooking time. In a convection oven the amount of food does not matter and food is cooked and browned very evenly. Combined convection and microwave

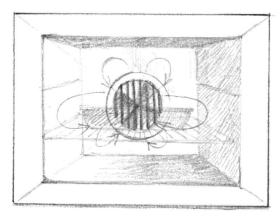

Fan circulates hot air for even, time-saving cooking.

Comparison Chart: Convection/Conventional Ovens

Food	Conventional Temperature	Time	Convection Temperature	Time
Meatloaf	180°C	1 hr	160°C	1 hr
Baked Potatoes	210°C	1 hr	190°C	40–50
Tuna Casserole	190°C	30 mins	180°C	30mins
Bread	190°C	50 mins	160°C	30–40 mins
Cake Mix	180°C	30–35 mins	140°C	40–45 mins
Quiche Pastry	200°C	10 mins	190°C	10 mins

ovens are now available to provide speed and evenness of cooking as well as browning. For most baking and roasting, the convection oven does not require preheating.

You will find with a convection oven that:

- foods with raising agents, such as yeast, air and baking powder, will rise higher because of the constant even oven temperature.

- roasting meats lose very little juice because they are seared all over very quickly, sealing all the juices in.

- most convection ovens can be set on *very* low temperatures, about 50°C, for proving yeast products evenly.

Convection Oven Recipes to Try

Raisin Breakfast Bread

Ingredients

50 g raisins
125 ml boiling water
25 g white cooking fat
1 tsp vanilla
75 g sugar
1 egg
150 g flour
1½ tsp baking powder
25 g chopped walnuts

Method

1 Place raisins in a small bowl. Pour boiling water over and let stand until cool.
2 In a large bowl, beat white cooking fat and vanilla until creamy. Gradually add sugar, beating until light and fluffy.
3 Add eggs one at a time, beating well after each addition.
4 In another bowl, combine flour and baking powder. Add flour mixture to creamed mixture alternately with raisin and water mixture. Mix thoroughly after each addition.
5 Stir in nuts. Spread in a greased flour-dusted 10 cm × 20 cm loaf tin. Bake at 160°C in convection oven for 1–1¼ hrs. Allow to cool slightly in pan.

Swiss Custard Ramekins

Ingredients

4 slices day-old firm white bread
margarine to spread bread
100 g grated cheese
2 eggs
150 ml milk
100 ml unsweetened apple juice
⅛ tsp dry mustard
2 spring onions (including tops), finely chopped

Method

1 Spread bread with butter and place in four well-buttered ramekins (150 ml).
2 Distribute cheese over each bread slice.
3 Beat eggs with half of the juice and add mustard.
4 Add mixture and the rest of the juice.
5 Pour egg mixture over cheese and sprinkle with onions. Cover and refrigerate for 10 mins.
6 Bake uncovered at 180°C in convection oven for 20–30 mins or until custard is set and puffed up.

Serves 4.

Hot Tuna Sandwiches

Ingredients

3 tbsp mayonnaise
3 tbsp chutney
1 tbsp French mustard
¼ tsp garlic salt
⅛ tsp pepper
6 hamburger buns
1 can tuna, drained
75 g grated cheddar cheese
50 g chopped green pepper
50 g chopped celery
¼ thinly sliced spring onion
3 chopped stuffed olives

Method

1 In a bowl, mix together mayonnaise, chutney, mustard, salt and pepper. Add tuna, cheese, green pepper, celery, onions and olives and mix well.
2 Split rolls in half. Spread equal amounts of tuna mixture on the bottom half of each roll. Cover with top half of roll.
3 Wrap each sandwich in foil. Refrigerate until an hour before required.

4 Allow rolls to stand at room temperature for 20 mins if they have been refrigerated, then bake in a convection oven at 180°C for 20 mins, or until the cheese melts and the sandwiches are heated through.

Serves 6.

Note: A good recipe for classes on consecutive days.

Sesame or Almond Baked Fish

A dusting of sesame seeds or sliced almonds enhances almost any baked fish. You can use just about any favourite: cod, haddock, whiting and coley are among the many possibilities.

Ingredients

4 fish fillets or steaks, each 10–20 mm thick
paprika
2 tbsp flour
50 g margarine
2 tbsp oil
25 g sesame seeds or sliced almonds
4 lemon wedges

Method

1 Wipe fish with damp cloth. Put a shallow, ovenproof dish, large enough to hold fish in a single layer, in convection oven while it pre-heats to 200°C. Lightly sprinkle fish with paprika, then coat with flour, shake off excess.
2 Remove dish from oven. Add margarine and oil to dish and swirl until margarine melts (fat should be about 10 mm deep). Lay fish in pan and turn to coat with melted margarine. Sprinkle evenly with sesame seeds or almonds.
3 Bake uncovered in convection oven for 10–12 mins or until fish flakes readily when prodded in thickest portion with a fork. Garnish with lemon.

Serves 4.

Baked Chutney Chicken

Ingredients

4 chicken pieces
75 ml soy sauce
3 tbsp chutney
parsley sprigs

Method

1 Rinse chicken pieces and pat dry Place chicken in a bowl and pour soy sauce over pieces. Let stand for about 15 mins, turning often.
2 Lift chicken pieces from bowl and arrange skin side up in single layer in a shallow dish. Brush evenly with chutney (finely chop large pieces).
3 Bake, uncovered, in convection oven at 180°C for 45–50 mins or until meat near thigh bone is no longer pink when slashed.
4 Arrange chicken on a plate, garnish with parsley.

Serves 4.

Resource Saver No. 7 Appliances

Refrigerator and Freezer

The advantages of home freezing and bulk buying are now appreciated by most people in our community. The home freezer can combine the long-term storage of fresh foods and the short-term storage of cooked foods and leftovers. Everyone in the family will know how valuable the refrigerator is. Almost as essential as a cooker, and combined with the freezer, it is an invaluable resource saver both in terms of saving shopping time and saving food and, therefore, money.

How long can food be kept in the freezer?

There's no hard and fast answer. The nature of the food and care in preparing, packaging and freezing are influential factors, but you can keep many foods up to one year. Some will store properly for only three to six months. No complete list can be given, but the following table can be used as a general guide.

Item	Maximum recommended storage (months)
Meats	
Lean fresh meat	8–9
Fatty meats (pork, etc.)	4–5
Seasoned fresh meats, salt meats	1–1½
Offal	3
Poultry (unstuffed)	6–12
Turkey	6–12
Fish	
Shell fish	1
Oily fish	3
White fish	6
Dairy products	
Unsalted butter	6
Salted butter	3
Cheese	6
Eggs (separated)	5–10
Fruits, vegetables and juices	12
Yeast, bread and rolls	
Baked	4–6 weeks
Unbaked	5–8 weeks

Item	Maximum recommended storage (months)
Sandwiches and scones	
Sandwiches	4–6 weeks
Scones—baked	1–2
Cakes	
Butter—baked	3–4
Butter—unbaked	2
Sponge—baked	3–4
Fruit cake—baked	6
Fruit cake—unbaked	3
Biscuits—baked	4–6
Biscuits—unbaked	2
Pies	
Baked	6
Unbaked	2
Stews, soups and other pre-cooked frozen foods	6
Such foods containing onion and garlic	2

(This table was developed by The Electricity Council)

Small Appliances

Most small appliances are designed to save human energy and time. However, they do not often save electricity or money. Some are merely gadgets and many are relatively expensive to buy and operate. Values need to be ranked in order of priority when decisions are being made to buy or not to buy. Which is of the most value — time or money, fuel or time, social pressure or money?

Any appliance with a heating element is power-expensive.

There are many more appliances. The appliances on page 56 are amongst those most commonly used in homes which can be seen as resource savers.

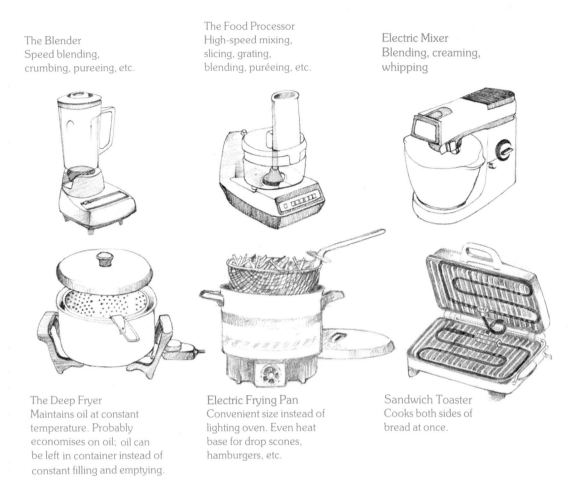

The Blender
Speed blending,
crumbing, pureeing, etc.

The Food Processor
High-speed mixing,
slicing, grating,
blending, puréeing, etc.

Electric Mixer
Blending, creaming,
whipping

The Deep Fryer
Maintains oil at constant
temperature. Probably
economises on oil; oil can
be left in container instead of
constant filling and emptying.

Electric Frying Pan
Convenient size instead of
lighting oven. Even heat
base for drop scones,
hamburgers, etc.

Sandwich Toaster
Cooks both sides of
bread at once.

Workshop

1 Prepare a selection of recipes using pressure cookers. Divide the
cooking time by four and judge whether it is sufficient to cook the dish.
Record your results for use in the future.

2 Cook three chicken joints—one in a baking dish with a little fat in a
conventional oven, one in the same oven on the same shelf but in an
oven bag, and one on a rotisserie (if available). Compare the results in
relation to cooking time, appearance of the product, crispness of the
skin and juiciness. Make decisions about the most desirable way for
your family to cook a chicken.

Investigation No. 10
Risen Products

Aim
- To compare risen products from conventional and convection ovens (or gas and electric)

Procedure

a Using the **Poppy Seed Plait** recipe (see page 44), make up two identical loaves. Cook one in a conventional oven and one in a convection oven. Use exactly the same sized tin for each loaf.

b Bake the loaves. Weigh each loaf as soon as it comes from the oven. Record the weight.

c Measure the circumference of each loaf around the girth and lengthwise.

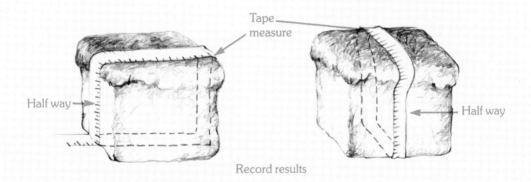

Tape measure

Half way

Half way

Record results

d Slice each loaf near the half-way mark. Examine the texture for size of air holes, size of crumb, moistness, etc. Record.

e Measure the height of each loaf and record results.

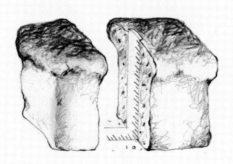

f   Answer the following questions.
   — Was the weight of the larger loaf any different?
   — Was there any difference in the texture?
   — How can you explain the results (consider the theory you studied relating to the heat in convection ovens).
   — What variables must be taken into account when doing an experiment like this, that is, how many *different* things might influence the results?

Conclusion

   — Can you draw any real conclusions by comparing these two loaves?
   — Could you be more definite about your results if the whole class worked in pairs and each pair did the experiment?
   — Why not try this by comparing the results from two loaves with the combined results of the whole class. Can you generalise about the quality of risen products in convection ovens?

Note: This exercise is an important one for understanding the limitations of research. If no convection ovens are available, do the exercise comparing gas and electric ovens.

Investigation No. 11
Managing Equipment

Aim

● To compare three different pieces of food preparation equipment in relation to
   — the quality of the apple purée produced
   — the time involved in the puréeing process

Procedure

a   Prepare and stew eight apples (see **Stewed Apple** recipe page 109) in the microwave oven, or just stew them in a saucepan.

b   Divide the apple into three equal-sized samples, each with equal pulp and equal juice.

c   Purée one sample in the food processor, one sample in the blender, and one sample through a sieve with a wooden spoon. (See Glossary on page 197 for definition of **pureé**).

d   Record the time taken for each method.

e   Measure each sample in a measuring jug. Record the level.

f   Observe each sample and rate for evenness and smoothness of purée. Record your rating with a tick in a table like the one below.

Sample	Very Good 1	2	3	4	Poor 5
1					
2					
3					

g   Remove 1 teaspoon of each sample and taste. A purée should be very smooth and completely free of pieces (lumps). Rate in a table as above.

h   Compile class averages for all ratings and recordings in a table like the one below.

Sample	Time	Measure	Observation	Taste
1				
2				
3				

i   Answer the following questions.
   — Which sample yielded the greatest amount of purée?
   — Which equipment yielded the better product? (How will you decide this?)
   — Which equipment saved the greatest amount of time?
   — What would influence your decision regarding the type of equipment to use if you had all the equipment available for the task?

Food Processor Recipes to Try

Creamy Chicken and Bacon Pâté

Ingredients

250 g chicken livers, fatty threads removed
1 small chopped bacon rasher, rind removed
1 small chopped onion
1 clove garlic
1 tbsp cream cheese
1 tbsp plain yoghurt
60 g margarine
freshly ground pepper

Method

1   Cut livers in half.
2   Cook bacon a few minutes in its own fat, add onion and garlic and cook until soft.
3   Discard garlic and place bacon and onion in processor with metal blade.
4   Using same saucepan, sauté livers a few at a time until just cooked but still pink inside.
5   Add to processor and blend.

6 With motor running, through food funnel add cheese, yoghurt and margarine cut into pieces. Blend.

7 Add ground pepper to taste.

8 Place in containers and seal well. If serving straight away make fancy pattern on top and garnish with parsley.

Broccoli Soup

Ingredients

375 g broccoli heads
500 ml chicken stock (or 500 ml water: 1 chicken stock cube)
2 tbsp cream
pepper to taste
parmesan cheese (optional)

Method

1 Boil stock, add broccoli, cook until tender (about 15 mins).

2 Lift broccoli from stock with draining spoon and place in processor. Blend with metal blade.

3 Return to stock, reheat, add pepper if necessary.

4 Stir in cream before serving but do not allow to boil.

5 Serve garnished with cheese.

Crunchy Vegetable Risotto

Ingredients

100 g brown rice
1 onion peeled
2 carrots, peeled
1 red pepper, seeds removed
100 g mushrooms
50 g peas
1 stick celery
1 tbsp oil
pepper
50 g cheese, grated
1 tbsp chopped parsley

Method

1 Cook the rice in boiling salted water until tender, about 30 minutes. Drain and keep hot.

2 Fit the slicing disc on the food processor and slice the onions, carrots, celery and pepper. Slice the mushrooms separately.

3 Fry the onion, carrot, celery and pepper in a deep, frying pan until they are just cooked.

4 Add the mushrooms, peas and cooked rice and cook for a few minutes.

5 Serve sprinkled with grated cheese and chopped parsley.

Serves 4.

Strawberry and Lime Fizzy

Ingredients

100 g strawberries, rinsed and hulled
125 ml cold soda water
3 tbsp lime juice (or lemon juice)
3 tbsp lime cordial
3 ice cubes

Method

1 With metal blade in processor, blend strawberries.

2 Add soda water, juice and cordial. Add ice cubes through funnel with motor in motion.

3 Pour into tall chilled glasses, garnish with a strawberry slice.

Resource Saver Recipes to Try

Farmhouse Pasty

Pastry Ingredients

200 g wholemeal flour
100 g margarine
2 tbsp water (approx.)

Filling Ingredients

1 tbsp oil
1 diced onion
1 crushed clove garlic
4 chopped mushrooms
150 g minced beef
½ beaten egg
1 tbsp chopped parsley
50 g grated cheese
a little salt and pepper

Method

1 Rub margarine into flour with fingertips until mixture resembles bread crumbs,.

2 Mix to a stiff dough with the water—this pastry must not be sticky.

3 Knead lightly and leave to rest while you prepare filling.

4 Heat oil. Fry vegetables lightly. Lift out of oil and drain.

5 Add meat to oil and fry until changed in colour all over—mix and mash during cooking to separate pieces.

6 Remove from heat and allow to cool, add vegetables, egg and cheese, salt and pepper if desired. Allow to cool a little.

7 Grease a Swiss roll tin. Roll pastry into a rectangle about 20cm × 60 cm. Trim edges to a neat shape. Keep scraps.

8 Pile cooled filling on one end of pastry leaving approximately 2–5 cm clear around edge.

9 Roll out scraps and cut out leaves, to decorate top. Make steam holes in pastry. Glaze with egg and water mixture. Bake at 200°C, gas mark 6 for 30 mins.

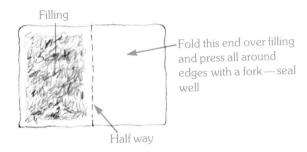

Filling

Fold this end over filling and press all around edges with a fork—seal well

Half way

Questions about the recipe

a In what way is this recipe a resource saver?

b What vegetables could you use as alternatives to onions and mushrooms?

c Would the recipe be more economical with less meat and more vegetables? Would it be as nutritious? Explain your answers.

d How could you change this recipe to suit a vegetarian?

Courgette and Tuna

Ingredients

3 medium courgettes, sliced
198 g can tuna
120 g mushrooms, sliced
100 ml water
1 chicken stock cube *or*
1 tsp soya sauce
1 onion, chopped

Method

1 Put all ingredients into a saucepan and simmer for 10 mins.

2 Serve with rice or potato crisps
Serves 4.

Questions about the recipe

a How much did the recipe cost per serving?

b How long did the recipe take to prepare and serve?

c In what ways is this recipe a resource saver?

Chicken Combination

Ingredients

2 tbsp flour
1 chicken stock cube
¼ tsp white pepper
½ tsp dried tarragon
4 chicken joints
4 medium potatoes
1 large onion
1 green pepper
3 medium carrots
375 ml water
2 tbsp low-fat plain yoghurt
finely chopped parsley
1 roasting bag

Method

1 Scrub and prick potatoes and place on tray in oven at 180°C/gas mark 4.

2 Mix flour, pepper and tarragon and coat chicken joints. Reserve any remaining flour.

3 Place chicken in roasting bag.

4 Slice onion, seed and slice green pepper and slice carrot.

5 Blend remaining flour with water and add crumbled cube.

6 Remove tray with potatoes from oven. Arrange potatoes along one end or one in each corner of tray. Place bag and chicken on tray. Place vegetables over chicken then pour over the stock, holding bag opening up to retain liquid.

7 Tie bag securely. Make 3 or 4 holes in top of bag at tie end.

8 Return tray to oven for 50 mins.

9 Transfer cooked chicken and vegetables to serving dish and return potatoes to oven.

10 Add liquid from bag to a saucepan, add parsley and yoghurt. Mix well and reheat without boiling. Spoon over chicken. Serve with potatoes.

Serves 4.

Questions about the recipe

a As you are only using one shelf in the oven, what else could you cook in the oven at the same time?

b In what ways is the recipe a resource saver?

Meat and Vegetable Stew (Qormeh Sabzi — Iran)

Ingredients

1½ tbsp oil
250 g boned shoulder of lamb, diced 1 cm
1 onion, chopped
pinch freshly ground black pepper
¼ tsp turmeric
2 tbsp lemon juice
125 ml water
1 tomato
5 spring onions, thinly sliced
1 tbsp finely chopped celery leaves
125 g spinach, chopped coarsely
1 tbsp chopped parsley
500 g tinned chick peas

Method

1 Heat 1 tbsp oil in pan and sauté lamb until well browned on all sides.

2 Add onion and sauté until soft.

3 Add pepper, turmeric, lemon juice and water and bring to boil.

4 Simmer covered for 15 mins.

5 Heat remaining oil and sauté spring onions, celery leaves, spinach and parsley for 2 mins. Stir

constantly. Add these vegetables and chick peas to meat and combine thoroughly.

6 Simmer for 20 mins. Serve garnished with wedges of raw tomato.

Serves 4.

Questions about the recipe

a If you replaced the chick peas with a can of tiny potatoes, would the recipe still 'work'?

b In what ways is the recipe a resource saver?

All-in-the-Oven Meals

MENU 1
Chicken
Combination
page 62
Old Fashioned
Tomato and Onion
Pie, page 31
Pears Ruby page 176

MENU 2
Fish Spirals, page
164
Stuffed Courgette
page 173
Brown Betty Flake
page 51

MENU 3
Baked Chutney
Chicken, page 54
Fresh Cauliflower au
Gratin, page 48
Jacket Potato, page 114
Orange Soufflé, page
175

MENU 4
Lemon Plaice, page
101
Pommes Gratinées,
page 114
Apple Raisin Pie,
page 125

MENU 5
Sesame or Almond
Baked Fish, page 54
Minted Carrots, page
51
Rhubarb and Apple
Crumble, page 174

● Work out two or three 'All-in-the-Oven' menus of your own, using recipes in this book or family favourites.

Part 2

◇

Finding Out About Food Needs

4 Food Needs

Why Do I Eat?

You eat generally to satisfy your **thirst** and your **hunger**. Your body regulates both these needs.

Thirst is regulated by the amount of water in the blood. Water is lost from the body via the lungs in the air you breathe out; via the kidneys as urine; and through the pores of your skin as sweat. When more than the usual amount of water is lost, such as through perspiration, the brain triggers a thirst sensation in the throat and general mouth area.

Hunger is felt as a tightness and rumbling in the central stomach area. This is thought to be regulated by the amount of glucose (a simple sugar) available in your bloodstream. If there is too little glucose the muscles in the stomach walls contract (tighten).

Hunger should not be confused with **appetite**. Appetite is more complex than hunger. It is influenced by the way you have

Thirst Regulation

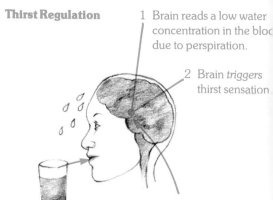

1 Brain reads a low water concentration in the bloo due to perspiration.

2 Brain *triggers* thirst sensation

3 Water is taken in to overcome the discomfort of thirst.

4 Feed-back sign turns off thirst centre.

Hunger Regulation

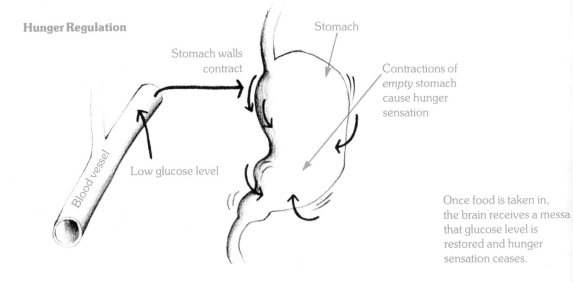

Stomach walls contract

Stomach

Contractions of *empty* stomach cause hunger sensation

Blood vessel

Low glucose level

Once food is taken in, the brain receives a messa that glucose level is restored and hunger sensation ceases.

been socialised in the family and in the community in which you live.

There are, however, many other reasons *why* you eat other than hunger and thirst. As you know, you sometimes eat when you are *not* thirsty or hungry. Many of the other reasons for eating are related to your patterns of behaviour and can be classed as being **social** and **cultural** reasons.

• Discuss what is meant by **social** and **cultural**. Did you arrive at an answer similar to this:

It is not always easy to separate the two, but generally, **social** relates to your day-to-day activities, people you meet, places you go, etc. That is, *where* you are and *with whom*. **Cultural** relates to the *way* you behave and relate to others, the spacing between your meals and *what* you eat.

Workshop

1 a Discuss how your activities yesterday might have influenced your eating behaviour.
  b Compare your eating behaviour on a school day with that of a Saturday or a Sunday. How do you account for your eating patterns?
2 a Make three lists of foods: one suitable for your next party; one for tonight's family meal; and one for tomorrow morning's breakfast for the family. Read through each list and write three adjectives at the base of each list to record your feelings about the foods.
  b Compare (how are they similar) and contrast (how do they differ) your answers with those of the rest of the class. What reasons are there for
    — any differences in your feelings?
    — any differences in the lists of food and feelings in the class?

How Does My Body Use Food?

You know that you must eat to stay alive and that what you eat influences your health. But do you really understand how this happens? Food not only forms and renews (builds and repairs) body parts, but it is necessary to carry out body functions.

Biologically then, food serves two main purposes:

• Food forms and renews the human body.
• Food is converted to the energy needed to carry out body functions.

How Does Food Form the Body?

What are you aware of about the eating process? Chewing, swallowing, hunger, the discomfort of overeating and the excretion of waste will all be familiar to you. But what actually *happens* to the food you eat?

The body breaks food down into small parts, or single molecules, which are then absorbed into the body cells for use.

Digestion and Absorption of Food

Mouth Food is chewed and mixed with saliva. Carbohydrate digestion commences.
Oesophagus Food is moved along to the

stomach by muscular movements called peristalsis.

Stomach Food is chewed, mixed with gastric juices and acid and turned into a kind of paste called chyme. There are very few changes to nutrients. Carbohydrate foods (sugars and starches) will spend the least time in the stomach, protein more and fats the most.

Duodenum Enzymes from the pancreas help to break up the carbohydrate, protein and fat molecules. Bile from the liver emulsifies fat (makes the molecules smaller).

- The substances that bring about most of the changes in foods in all parts of the digestive system are called **enzymes**.

Small Intestine More digestive juices and enzymes are added and foods are broken down into tiny molecules that can be absorbed through the walls of the small intestine into the blood. The blood carries these food molecules—fatty acids (fats), amino acids (proteins) and glucose (carbohydrates) as well as vitamins and minerals — to the cells so that *new cells can be produced, old cells replaced** and so that there is the *energy for the cells to function*. These three activities are called **growth**.

Large Intestine Unusable food[†] is pushed along and usable water is extracted. This is filtered by the kidneys and the waste excreted in the urine.

Rectum   Solid waste is expelled as faeces.

---

* Cells not only differ in function, they also differ in lifespan. For example, the cells lining the intestine are replaced daily, the red blood cells every four months and the liver cells every eighteen months, whereas muscle cells and most nerve cells last for the human lifespan.

† Much of the unusable food is cellulose (fibre) which is an indigestible carbohydrate. Cellulose has the ability to absorb water and helps to keep the faeces soft and easily moved. Too much strain in the large intestine can lead to damage of this important organ.

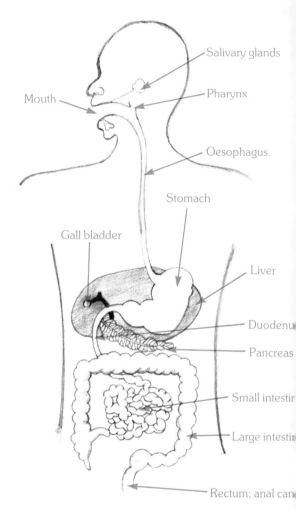

Salivary glands

Mouth

Pharynx

Oesophagus

Stomach

Gall bladder

Liver

Duodenum

Pancreas

Small intestine

Large intestine

Rectum; anal canal

The process through which the body receives and uses the materials necessary to form and renew body parts, enabling them to carry out their functions, is known as **nutrition**. The substances in food which perform body functions are called **nutrients** (see page 74 for a table of nutrients and their functions). These many different nutrients combine to form the various parts of the body.

- How is your body made up? How different are all the body cells?

- If you just look at your hands you will find a large number of the answers to these questions. With your eyes you can see *three* main types of cells on your hands:

The Building of Body Tissues

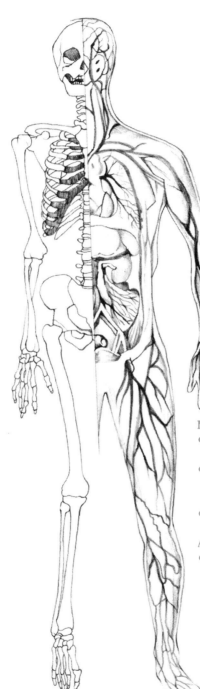

The Hard Tissues

- Bone
- Teeth
- Cartilage (in nose, ears and around ends of bone)

The Soft Tissues

- *Skin* covers and lines all parts of the body
- *Connective Tissue* supports and binds organs, cells, etc.
- *Muscle* enables movement and produces heat as a result
- *Nerve Tissue* conducts impulses

Nutrients Involved:

- *All nutrients required as for soft tissues* (see opposite)

Plus:

- *Calcium* and
- *Phosphorus* to harden bones and teeth
- *Fluoride* to maintain hardness in bones and teeth
- *Vitamin A* for normal bone and teeth development
- *Vitamin D* to enable the body to use calcium and phosphorus

And:

- The *Energy* needed to produce the nerve cells (see opposite)

Nutrients Involved:

- *Proteins* (amino acids) to form new cells
- *Vitamin C* (ascorbic acid) for the formation of connective tissue
- *Water* is essential in all cells and around all cells

And:

- The *Energy* needed to build the tissues. This comes from:
    - *Carbohydrate* energy
    - *Fat* energy
    - *Vitamin B Complex* to enable the energy to get into cells and be used
    - *Iron* to carry oxygen which must be present for energy to be used

those that make up the skin, those that make up the hair; and those that make up the nails. Now feel your hands. Touch one hand very lightly with the other — what you feel is soft. Now press one of your fingers between the thumb and forefinger of the other hand. It is quite obvious that it is not soft all the way through, something hard, which you know to be bone, is holding your finger in shape.

The whole body is made up of hard tissue and soft tissue. Different nutrients combine to make up these tissues. If you tap your teeth with your fingernail and then tap your cheek, it is obvious that they are made of different materials.

How Does the Body Use Energy?

What is energy?
- Discuss this as a class and develop a definition of energy.
- Think about your body. How warm do you feel right now? Take your temperature and record. Carry out an activity, for example, jog for five minutes, step up and down on a chair seat twenty times or skip for one minute. How warm do you feel now? Take your temperature and record. Was there any difference in the temperature? If not, can you explain why?

What you probably noticed was that your body lost heat but its temperature stayed constant. Your skin felt warmer after an activity but soon returned to normal. Your skin, regulated by the brain, controls body temperature. When you expend lots of energy by being very active, heat is given off. The blood is pumped around faster and travels quickly to the skin where it is cooled off by the atmosphere. Needless to say, you cool off more quickly in cool weather. Heat is, therefore, a by-product of energy usage.

You have just learnt from the brief outline of the digestion of food that some foods are broken down into energy-giving molecules and in the diagram on page 69 energy is shown as being needed to build the body. The body can not only retrieve food energy, but it can store it for later use in the muscles, liver and fatty deposits of the body. You will learn in Investigation No. 12 how the nutrients get into the cells. In much the same way, the essential oxygen is carried by the iron in the blood, and enters the cells. Cells further break up energy nutrients, combine them with oxygen and are then able to release energy.

The body is generally very economical in the way it uses energy, releasing it in small bursts so that it is not wasted. If you leave a tap running continuously when, say, washing a vegetable, you waste a great deal of water. The same thing applies to energy. If your body released energy in a continuous stream much of it would be wasted. You vary in your needs from one minute to another.

When you began this section on energy, you were asked to perform an activity, that is, burn up some energy quickly. How did your breathing change after this activity? How long was it before your breathing returned to normal? The reason your breathing speeds up is so that your body can keep up the supply of oxygen that is necessary to combine with the energy nutrients. The fitter your body is, the more used to exercise you are, the faster your breathing returns to normal and the more vigorous the exercise you are able to tolerate.

Investigation No. 12
Absorption

Aim
- To develop an understanding of how food molecules reach cells to perform their function

Procedure

a Prepare an experiment as shown in the diagram below. Imagine that the membrane containing the salt solution is a cell containing various concentrations of substances. After a while you will notice that the level will rise up the capillary tube. Why do you think this happens? This action is called **osmosis**.

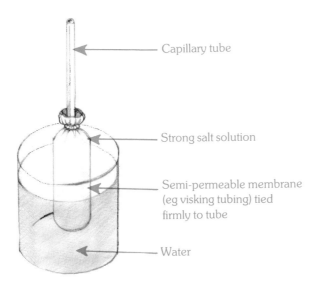

Capillary tube

Strong salt solution

Semi-permeable membrane (eg visking tubing) tied firmly to tube

Water

b Fill a glass with water and imagine that it is a cell. Add a drop or two of red colouring. Do not move the glass. What happens to the colouring? This action is called **diffusion**. It happens because molecules are constantly moving and they spread (diffuse) the colouring.

Conclusion

- What happens to food molecules when they enter a cell?
- How do food molecules get from the intestine to the blood and from the blood to a cell?

Investigation No. 13
Cellulose

Aim

- To discover the digestibility of cellulose

Procedure

a Collect some apple skin, celery strings and bran from wheat.

b Try to dissolve them in cold water.

c Try to dissolve them in boiling water.

d Boil them in a dilute acid solution (for example, cream of tartar or vinegar).

e Now try a ten per cent acid solution and heat.

f Next try to dissolve them in a dilute alkaline solution (for example, bicarbonate of soda).

g Boil up the samples with a ten per cent alkaline solution.

h Record the results of all the previous steps.

Conclusion

— As digestive juices are either acidic or alkaline what conclusions can you make?

Note: The acids and alkali suggested for use are safe and readily available in the Home Economics Room. Teachers may wish to substitute hydrochloric acid and caustic soda but dilute solutions must be used and care must be taken.

How Do I Know What is in Food?

There are, of course, exceptions to the rule and different vitamins and minerals are found in different foods. The main exception to the rule centres around the fact that there are two different sources of protein. These are:

- animal sources
- vegetable sources

As stated previously in the section on digestion, proteins are made up of amino acids. There are about twenty known amino acids, 8 of which must be supplied in our food if life is to be maintained. These 8 are called *essential* amino acids, because it is *essential*

that we get them from food. The others can be made by the body if necessary.

The following foods contain all 8 essential amino acids necessary to support life: meat, fish, eggs, cheese, yoghurt, milk, soya beans. Their proteins are of high quality.

Some sources of low quality proteins do not contain sufficient quantities of essential amino acids to support life if eaten alone. Foods containing insufficient quantities of essential amino acids are legumes (dried peas, beans and lentils), nuts, cereals and small amounts in vegetables. Most fruits are not good sources of protein.

Note: The body can turn fat to glucose, carbohydrate to fat, and protein to glucose or fat, but it must get essential protein from food.

As a general rule:

Animal foods, seeds, nuts =
fats, protein, vitamins, minerals

Animal foods
= fats, vitamins,
minerals

Plants = carbohydrate
(including
fibre), vitamins,
minerals

How to improve protein value.

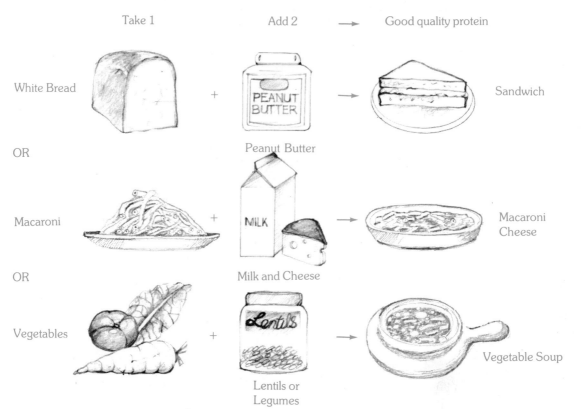

Take 1   Add 2   ⟶   Good quality protein

White Bread + PEANUT BUTTER ⟶ Sandwich

OR

Peanut Butter

Macaroni + MILK ⟶ Macaroni Cheese

OR

Milk and Cheese

Vegetables + Lentils ⟶ Vegetable Soup

Lentils or Legumes

Constantly referring to nutrient tables, such as the one that follows, is the best way to develop a more detailed understanding of what is in food and the function it performs in your body. By using such a table it can soon be discovered that the body needs a variety of nutrients all at once. We must, therefore, choose a variety of foods at each meal.

Nutrient	Source	Function in body
Carbohydrate	Cereals, vegetables and fruits are best sources. Foods such as cakes, sweets, biscuits, cordials, syrups, sugars, honey and jam contain large amounts but little of other nutrients in proportion to their sugar content, and little or no fibre.	Major source of energy Essential for normal cells — necessary for protein to be used properly Fibre is an indigestible carbohydrate that provides bulk to the diet, helping to prevent diseases of the large intestine (pectin in fruit and agar in seaweed are indigestible carbohydrates with similar properties)

Nutrient	Source	Function in body
Protein	High quality: meat, milk, cheese, yoghurt, fish, eggs, soya beans low quality: nuts, cereals, vegetables	Necessary to build all new cells (synthesis) — life depends on protein Enzymes are proteins Hormones (body regulators) are usually proteins Forms antibodies in the blood to defend the body against infection
Fat	Large amounts: butter, margarine, dripping, lard, oils, cream. Average amounts: egg yolk, meat, dairy foods (except butter and cream), fish, nuts Small amounts: some fruits, vegetables, cereals	Provide the body with fat soluble vitamins A, D, E, K A very rich supply of energy Forms a protective pad around vital organs, e.g. heart Pads pressure points of the body, e.g. heels, buttocks, fingertips Some hormones are fatty substances Helps in cell functions
Water (not a nutrient but an essential substance for life — second only to air in importance)	All drinks, fruit, vegetables, meat, dairy foods, cooked cereal products	Essential for all body fluids Essential for hormonal activity Essential for digestion and absorption of nutrients Solvent for waste products
Vitamin A	Cod liver oil, cheese, liver, carrots, green leafy vegetables, apricots, mango (on a normal varied diet deficiencies are rare)	For normal vision To keep the nasal passages moist Helps prevent respiratory infections Involved in growth
Vitamin B Complex 1 Thiamin	Marmite, yeast, legumes, green leafy vegetables, wholegrain cereals	Energy release from carbohydrates Healthy nervous system
2 Riboflavin	Milk, liver, marmite, yeast nuts, green vegetables	Involved in energy usage and cell respiration
3 Nicotinic acid	Marmite, yeast, legumes, peanuts, liver, kidney	Essential for a continual supply of energy to the cells Helps the body to use carbohydrate, protein and fat

Nutrient	Source	Function in body
4 Vitamin B$_6$	Widespread in foods (deficiencies rare)	Vital for the body's use of protein, and formation of haemoglobin. Important for brain function Involved in energy usage
5 Biotin	Egg yolk, liver, kidney, yeast, nuts. Produced in the intestine.	Essential for use of food in the body. Necessary for normal metabolism.
6 Pantothenic acid	Widespread in foods (deficiencies rare)	Essential for the body's use of carbohydrate and fat and, therefore, the release of energy
7 Folic acid	Yeast, meat, liver, green leafy vegetables, bananas and a wide variety of foods	Essential for normal cells Helps in usage of protein For the production of red blood cells
8 Vitamin B$_{12}$	Offal (e.g. kidneys, heart, tongue, liver), eggs, seafoods, dairy foods, yeast	Works with folic acid to produce red blood cells Essential for normal cells
Vitamin C (Ascorbic acid)	Fruits, green peppers, Brussels sprouts, potatoes, cabbage	Helps wound healing Helps prevent infection Essential for the formation of the connective tissue between body cells (collagen) Must be present so body can use folic acid Increases absorption of iron Protects vitamins A and E Important in hormone production
Vitamin D	Major source is the action of sunlight on the skin. Dietary sources are less significant but best sources are oily fish and cod liver oil	Influences balance of the hardness of bones and teeth with calcium and phosphorus
Calcium	Dairy foods, fish, green vegetables	For bone and teeth formation and hardening For muscle contraction Necessary for blood clotting Transmission of nerve impulses
Phosphorus	In most foods	Essential in all cells Essential in formation of hard tissue Essential in energy release

Iron	Prunes, red meat, green vegetables, bread, eggs, liver, wheatgerm, baby cereal	Transports oxygen to all body tissues Necessary for healthy blood
Potassium	Wheatgerm, branflakes, dried figs, prunes, sultanas, baked beans, haricot beans, milk, whitefish	Helps maintain the internal environment of the body Regulates heart beat Nerve impulse regulation Helps to get glucose into the cells for energy
Sodium	Common salt, take-away foods, packet mix soups and sauces, soya sauce, soup cubes, cured meats. Average intake of sodium is too high. This may encourage high blood pressure	Maintains osmotic pressure For nerve impulses Helps maintain internal environment of body Helps transport glucose into cells for energy
Iodine	Seafood, vegetables, iodised salt.	Essential in fluids outside cells (extra-cellular fluid). Essential part of the hormones produced by the thyroid gland. (see page 81)
Fluoride	Seafood, tea, some plant foods	Maintains hard bones and teeth
Magnesium	Peanuts, legumes, green vegetables	Important for enzyme activity Works with calcium and potassium. Involved with nerve and muscular activity.
Zinc	Eggs, wheat germ, roast beef, cheddar cheese, poultry, whole grain cereals	For normal foetal and infant growth For normal reproduction For wound healing

Workshop

1 Below is a day's menu for a patient in hospital:
   Breakfast: Rolled oats porridge, milk, steamed fish, toast and tea.
   Lunch: Bread, honey, an apple.
   Dinner: Steamed chicken, peas, carrot, potatoes, a fresh banana
                      water to drink.
   This menu has been carefully selected to keep one type of food as low
   as possible. Which type is this — carbohydrate, fat or protein?

2 A student has sandwiches spread with butter and honey followed by a chocolate bar for lunch. This is an unhealthy meal. What type of foods are missing?

3 How does milk in the diet help the growth of healthy bones in children?

4 Recall your lesson on digestion and note that carbohydrate is the fastest nutrient to be digested, protein the second fastest and fat the slowest. With this in mind, and with the information in the above tables, write an account of the fate of a meat pie after you have eaten it.

5 A hiker going on a four-day trip takes rolled oats, dried apricots and chocolates. Why would he pick these foods? Why would they provide an unsuitable diet for a longer period?

6 Look back at 'The Building of Body Tissue' diagram on page 69 and refer to the tables above. List every nutrient involved in the production and release of energy in the body. Plan a menu for yourself for one day that contains all these nutrients.

7 **Puzzle**
Discover the word which fits in these squares:

Each of the following words have at least four letters in common with it and help to define it.
    Repair, Antibody, Hormone, Synthesis

8 Examine the recipes following the next Investigation. Each one is suitable for a meal but would not be a really healthy meal on its own. Answer the questions at the end of each recipe. Prepare one of them and serve an accompaniment that will help to *balance out* the nutritive value of the meal.

Investigation No. 14
Identifying Nutrients
Aim

- To discover how to identify nutrients in food through scientific experiment

Procedure

a Collect very small portions of food such as flour, eggwhite, cheese, sugar, onions, potato, apple and milk. (Different groups could test different foods).

b Chop up and crush the solid food. Separate each type of food sample into four separate test-tubes with a little water. (Milk need not have water added.) Shake well and label for identification.

c To one of each food sample, boil the solution and let it cool. When it is cold add three or four drops of iodine solution. If the solution turns dark blue, starch (carbohydrate) is present.

---

d To one of each food sample dip a Clinistix strip into the solution. After *exactly* 10 seconds compare the colour of the strip with the colour on the label. Purple is positive for glucose and an unchanged pink negative.

e To one of each food add 8 to 10 drops of dilute sodium hydroxide solution. Leave to stand for 2 minutes. Then add 2 or 3 drops 1% copper sulphate solution to each food and leave to stand for at least 10 minutes. If the sample becomes a violet colour protein is present. This is called the Biuret Test. NB: Goggles should be worn. Copper sulphate is poisonous so hands should be thoroughly washed after using it. Sodium hydroxide is caustic and if accidentally splashed on the skin or clothes they should be rinsed with plenty of clean, cold water.

f Press half a teaspoon of the food on to a piece of filter paper. Scrape off and allow the paper to dry in a warm place. Hold the paper up to the light and if there is a grease spot the food contains fat.

g Draw up a chart like the one below for each food sample and record the results from the whole class.

Food name	Test for starch	Sugar	Protein	Fat

Put + for a positive result and − for a negative result in the appropriate columns.

Recipes to Try

The pastry in this recipe is not easy to handle. Perhaps you could answer the questions without actually making the dish.

Bacon and Egg Pie

Ingredients

1 quantity cream cheese pastry (recipe follows)
2 rashers bacon, chopped
4 spring onions, chopped
2 eggs
pepper to taste
125 g cream cheese, cut into cubes
beaten egg to glaze

Method

1 Roll out half the pastry and line the base and sides of a deep pie dish. Sprinkle with bacon and onion.

2 Break the eggs over the bacon and season with pepper. Arrange cheese over the eggs.

3 Roll out remaining pastry to cover pie, press into place and crimp edges. Make a few slits in the top for steam to escape and glaze with beaten egg. Bake at 200°C, gas mark 6 until pastry is crisp and golden, about 40 mins.

Serves 4−6.

Cream Cheese Pastry

Ingredients

150 g plain flour
125 g cream cheese, softened at room temperature
125 g margarine, softened

Method

1 Sift flour and gradually blend in the cream cheese and softened margarine until the dough is smooth.

2 Wrap in plastic film and chill for 1 hour before rolling out.

Questions about the recipe

a Which nutrient is over-represented in this recipe? Explain your answer.

b If you had this pie with salad for dinner what could you have for breakfast and lunch that day in an attempt to balance your diet?

Salmon Roll

Ingredients

212 g can pink salmon
1 tsp chopped parsley
¼ tsp tarragon
2 tsp lemon juice
a little pepper
200 g S.R. flour
50 g margarine
1 slightly beaten egg
125 ml milk

Method

1 Drain and flake salmon, removing any dark skin.

2 Mix in herbs, juice, and sprinkle with pepper. Set aside.

3 Sift flour, rub in the margarine until the mixture resembles fine breadcrumbs. Make a well in the centre, add egg and milk and mix to an elastic dough.

4 Knead lightly on a floured surface, roll out to a 1 cm thick oblong.

5 Cover with the salmon mixture leaving a margin. Brush milk over the margin, roll up as for a Swiss roll; tuck ends under.

6 Carefully lift on to a greased oven tray, brush with milk and make 3 or 4 slits along the top.

7 Bake in a hot oven (220°C, gas mark 7) for 15 mins, reduce to a moderate oven (180°C, gas mark 4) and cook for another 20 mins. Serve with parsley sauce.

Serves 4–6.

Parsley Sauce

Ingredients

25 g margarine
25 g flour
250 ml milk
pinch cayenne pepper
2 tbsp chopped parsley

Method

1 Melt margarine in a saucepan. Add flour and stir until smooth, cook 1 min (this is called a roux). Remove from the heat.

2 Add the liquid slowly, stirring constantly.

3 Return to the heat, bring to the boil stirring constantly.

4 Season with cayenne and cook 2–3 mins.

5 Fold in parsley.

Serve.

Questions about the recipe

a If you use wholemeal flour instead of white flour would you need to alter the recipe in any way?

b If you use wholemeal flour instead of white flour how would the nutritive value be altered?

c Suggest two accompaniments you could serve with the **Salmon Roll** to make it a healthier meal. Explain your choices.

How Much Food Do I Need?

Energy

How much money have you spent so far today? Compare your answer with those of the rest of the class. You will have found that each class member has spent a different amount of money . Likewise , the answers would all be different if asked about the amount of *energy* you have spent so far today. However, this is harder to measure. Different money has different values:

20p = 20p money valve

£1 = 100p

Money values are measured in pence (p) in Britain. The energy value of a food is measured in kilojoules (kJ) or kilocalories (kcal), and different foods have different energy (kilojoule/kilocalorie) values*

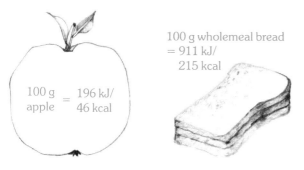

100 g wholemeal bread = 911 kJ/ 215 kcal

$\dfrac{100\ g}{apple} = \dfrac{196\ kJ/}{46\ kcal}$

The value of money is regulated by the government and by international values. The energy value of food depends on the amount of fat, carbohydrate and/or protein a food contains. Each of these three nutrients can produce energy, and the amount of energy each can produce varies from one to another. Fat produces the greatest amount of kilojoules per gram, while protein and carbohydrate are almost the same as each other and are a little less than half that of fat.

Energy Value of Nutrient

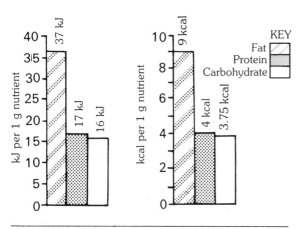

* You will find an extensive list of these values in McCance and Widdowson's *The Composition of Foods* by A A Paul and D A T Southgate (1978) HMSO

How much of this energy (that is, how many kilojoules or kilocalories) do you spend each day?

We can divide the energy the body needs into two categories:

● Involuntary energy;
● Voluntary energy.

Involuntary energy is the energy used to maintain all unconscious body activity:

● the functioning of the digestive system;
● the activity of the kidneys;
● the beating of the heart;
● the activity of the brain and nerves;
● activities of all other organs and glands.

This unconscious energy usage accounts for *more than half* of our total energy needs. The rate at which this energy is used in the body is called the Basal Metabolic Rate. The Basal Metabolic Rate (BMR), which can be defined as the amount of energy required to maintain the body while it is at rest, varies considerably from one person to another.

The main things that influence BMR are:

● Body type (size, shape and weight of an individual). There are three main body types, most of us are a mixture of two.

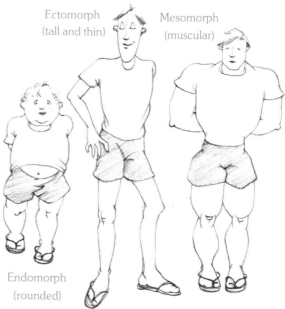

Ectomorph (tall and thin)   Mesomorph (muscular)

Endomorph (rounded)

- Sex. Males have a higher BMR than females.
- Age. Children have a higher BMR than adults.
- Rate of growth. Those growing have a higher rate (this includes pregnant women).
- Skin surface area. Greater amounts of energy are required to maintain body temperature in small bodies — a small body has a larger skin surface area to volume ratio and, therefore, there is a greater heat loss from the surface (see Investigation No. 14).

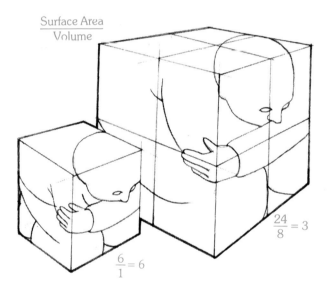

Surface Area / Volume

$$\frac{24}{8} = 3$$

$$\frac{6}{1} = 6$$

A small body, for example, a child, has a larger surface area to volume ratio than a large body, for example, an adult; thus, the rate of heat loss tends to be greater for the child and a higher metabolic rate is required in order to maintain body temperature.

There are three or four other influences such as food habits (what is eaten and when), climate, fever and medication, but they are not as influential as those above.

- Look at the main things that influence BMR, listed above. They have a common element, that is, there is something similar about all these influences. From a class discussion, see if you can come up with the words to complete the following sentence. Write the whole sentence in your book.

The BMR is virtually proportional to the . ... of the ....

Voluntary energy is the energy that you are more or less aware you are using. Next to basal metabolism, muscular activity accounts for the largest energy expenditure. The amount of energy needed for an activity such as playing tennis or studying for an exam depends on muscle movement, on the amount of weight being moved and on the length of time the activity is performed.

Remember in your introduction to energy on page 70 you discovered that heat is a by-product of energy usage. This gives you some indication of the amount of energy needed to carry out a task, although it cannot be relied upon completely. Remember that the heat you *feel* depends somewhat on the air temperature. For example, swimming racing and training is one of the most strenuous of sports but a swimmer probably does not feel as hot as a hiker. Also, a swimming race is usually much shorter in time than a hike.

Energy is also required to maintain your body temperature and to sustain growth. As the human body needs to be exercised, it is important to maintain a regular exercise programme which is balanced by the kilojoule or kilocalorie value of food consumed.

1050–1470 kJ (250–350 kcal) per hour

330–420 kJ (80–100 kcal) per hour

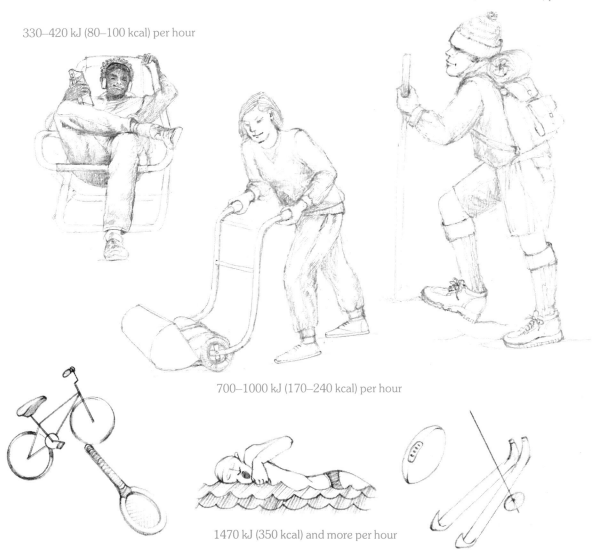

700–1000 kJ (170–240 kcal) per hour

1470 kJ (350 kcal) and more per hour

Workshop

1 Now we have looked at the body's need for energy you should be able
to complete the following equation:
Total energy needs = BMR + ...

2 Young children often eat as much as their parents who are twice their
size. Can you explain this?

Investigation No. 15
Surface Area vs Heat

Aim

- To determine the relationship of the skin surface area of the body to the Basal Metabolic Rate

Procedure

a You will need two containers with lids, each of the same volume and made of the same material, but one tall and one squat.

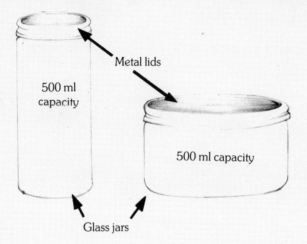

Fill each container with hot water and check the temperature with a thermometer from the centre of the water in the container and record. Place lids in position and set aside 30–40 minutes.

b Collect 16 wooden blocks, each of equal size and weight (children's play equipment).
Stack 2 piles of 8 blocks as shown in the diagram below.

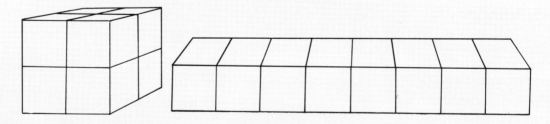

Estimate the surface area of each pile. Dismantle and weigh each pile (they should be the same).

c After you have left the jars for 30–40 minutes remove the lids and record the temperatures simultaneously. Estimate temperature loss in each jar.

Discussion/Conclusion

— Discuss differences in water temperatures.
— Compare surface areas of blocks.
— What decisions can you make about people of different heights but the same weight? Which type of person will require the most heat (energy) to maintain body temperature? How does skin surface area influence BMR?

Proportion

We need certain proportions of one nutrient to another—that is, the proportion of protein to carbohydrate, carbohydrate to fat and so on. The Healthy Diet Pyramid, shown on page 86, has been developed as a guide to help us determine these proportions. The Healthy Diet Pyramid does not specify amounts because we are all so different, rather it shows the *proportion* of different foods the body needs.

When you looked at the tables on pages 74–77 you would have realised that no one nutrient can work on its own for any purpose in the body. Therefore, all nutrients should be present in the body at the same time.

You will notice that the Healthy Diet Pyramid has classified foods into the following groups:

● Foods that we need the **most** which are our major source of carbohydrate energy, fibre and many vitamins and minerals.

● Foods that we should eat in **moderate** amounts which are particularly rich in completely proteins, some fats, vitamins and minerals.

● Foods that we should eat **least** which are rich in fat and sugar, both of which may be omitted from the diet provided the other two groups are taken in proportion to ensure the supply of fat soluble vitamins and carbohydrates.

The number of diet-related diseases in this country, for example, heart disease, diabetes, diseases of the colon and obesity, and alarming statistics such as the average annual consumption of sugar being 44 kg per person and the average daily consumption of meat being 150 g per person, prompted the development of dietary guidelines. It was basically from these guidelines that the Healthy Diet Pyramid evolved.

The Healthy Diet Pyramid

Tells us the proportion of food
we should eat.

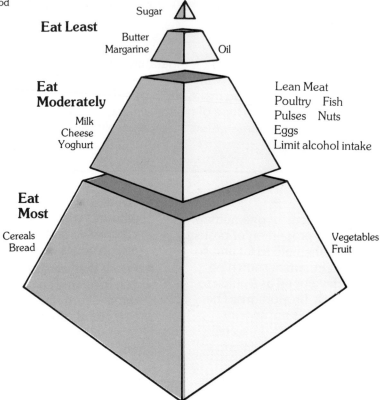

Sugar

Eat Least

Butter
Margarine   Oil

**Eat
Moderately**

Lean Meat
Poultry   Fish
Pulses   Nuts
Eggs
Limit alcohol intake

Milk
Cheese
Yoghurt

**Eat
Most**

Cereals
Bread

Vegetables
Fruit

Workshop

1 Look back at the table of nutrients on pages 74–77 and find out the
   following:
   a Which nutrient works with iron?
   b Which nutrients are necessary for us to be able to use protein
      properly?
   c Which two vitamins work together to produce red blood cells?
   d Which nutrients are necessary for healthy bone development?
2 Write a paragraph telling how activity 1 above helped you to
   understand the interrelationship of nutrients in the body.
3 Which of the following meals best represents the Healthy Diet
   Pyramid?
   a Grilled steak, potato chips, grilled tomato, minted peas. Bread and
      butter pudding.
   b Steamed fish, tossed salad, ratatouille. Rice pudding.
   c Roast lamb, roast potatoes, peas, minted carrots, gravy. Apple pie,
      custard and cream.

Dietary Guidelines

Eat less fat

Eat a variety of foods each day

Prevent and control obesity

Eat less sugar

Limit alcohol intake

Eat more fruit, vegetables, bread and cereals

Eat less salt

Drink more water

Encourage breast feeding

4 Plan a meal for a small group that applies the Healthy Diet Pyramid and is also low in salt, sugar and fat as recommended by the NACNE report. Select from the recipes at the end of this workshop and those elsewhere in this book.

Recipes to Try

Potato Soup

Ingredients

500 g potatoes
1 leek
1 or 2 cloves garlic
25 g margarine
900 ml stock or water
salt and pepper
pinch of nutmeg
chopped parsley

Method

1 Chop leek finely and fry gently in margarine with chopped potato and garlic for 10 mins.

2 Stir in stock, seasoning and nutmeg, simmer until potato is tender.

3 Put through blender or sieve. Reheat and check seasoning. Stir in the parsley. Serve with croutons (small squares of dry toast).

Tarragon Chicken

Ingredients

1 small chicken
3–4 small carrots
bay leaf
salt and pepper
parsley
1 tsp chopped tarragon
1 whole clove

Sauce

25 g margarine
25 g flour
250 ml stock (from the pot)
1 egg yolk
200 ml plain low-fat yoghurt
6 tarragon leaves (optional)

Method

1 Place the chicken in a pan of boiling water; the liquid should come half way up the chicken.

2 Add carrots, salt, pepper, bay leaf, parsley and 1 tsp chopped tarragon (a little less if using dried tarragon). Simmer for 1 hour.

3 12–15 mins before chicken is cooked, make the sauce. Melt the margarine in a small saucepan, do not let it colour. Add the flour and stir until absorbed gradually, add the stock stirring continuously. (The stock is taken from the chicken pan.)

4 Simmer for approximately 10 mins. Beat the egg yolks into the yoghurt, remove the sauce from heat, beat in the egg mixture vigorously.

5 Take chicken from the cooking pan and place on a hot serving dish, dip the tarragon leaves in hot water, then arrange on breast of chicken. Pour the sauce on top and serve immediately.

Serves 4.

Cheese and Potato Pie

Ingredients

450 g puff pastry
450 g potatoes
100 g chopped onions
3 cloves garlic
100 g grated cheese
1 egg
125 ml milk
chopped parsley

Method

1 Line a flan tin with pastry.

2 Slice potatoes very thinly and blanch for 3 mins in boiling water. Arrange potatoes, onions, garlic, grated cheese and seasoning in layers — each layer with salt and pepper. Pour in half the milk.

3 Cover with remaining pastry, pressing the edges together firmly. Make a hole in the centre and decorate the top. Beat together the egg and remaining milk. Brush some milk over the pastry. Bake at 220°C, gas mark 7 for 30–40 mins.

4 Stir parsley into remaining egg mixture and pour into the hole in the pastry. Return to oven for 5 mins. Serve hot.

Serves 4 or more.

Spicy Spareribs

Ingredients

500 g pork spareribs
3 tbsp tomato ketchup
1 clove garlic, crushed
2 tbsp brown sugar
2 tbsp soy sauce
1 medium onion, grated
2 shakes Chinese Five Spice powder
125 ml unsweetened orange juice

Method

1 Cover ribs with lightly salted water and simmer 30 mins. Drain and place in a shallow baking dish.

2 Combine remaining ingredients and spoon over pork.

3 Cover with foil or a lid and bake at 200°C, gas mark 6 for 20 mins, turning once. Remove cover and bake a further 20 mins or until brown and tender. Serve with boiled rice.

Serves 4.

Cauliflower Medley

Ingredients

½ medium-sized cauliflower
½ medium-sized red pepper
125 g mushrooms
25 g margarine
salt, pepper

Method

Break cauliflower into small florets, cut pepper into quarters, slice the quarters crosswise. Cut the prepared mushrooms into slices.

Cook the cauliflower in about 3 cm boiling water for 8–10 mins, or until tender, drain.

Gently fry the pepper in the margarine until barely tender, add the mushrooms and cook for a few minutes, or until just softened.

Mix in the cauliflower, salt and pepper, stir lightly, cook gently until reheated.

Serves 4.

Crumbed Green Beans

Ingredients

00 g green beans
clove garlic, crushed
¼ tsp pepper
25 ml low-fat plain yoghurt
00 g soft breadcrumbs
5 g melted margarine

Method

Cut beans into slices and cook in boiling, salted water, with garlic added, until just tender. Drain thoroughly, put into an ovenproof dish.

Stir seasoned pepper into the yoghurt, spoon over beans. Toss the crumbs in enough melted margarine to coat well, sprinkle over the yoghurt and bake in a moderate oven for 20 mins.

Serves 4.

Braised Red Cabbage

Ingredients

½ small red cabbage
½ medium-sized onion
Granny Smith apple
5 g margarine
tbsp sugar
tbsp wine vinegar
epper

Method

Shred cabbage finely, removing the hard stalks, wash well. Put into a pan with cold water to cover, slowly bring to boiling point, rinse in cold water, drain. Slice the peeled onion, peel, core and slice apples.

2 Melt margarine in a saucepan, add the sugar and cook gently until golden brown. Add onion and apples, cover, cook very gently for 3–4 mins.

3 Add the cabbage, stir well, pour the vinegar over and stir to mix through. Cover and simmer for 3–4 mins. Add 80 ml water, and pepper, cover tightly, braise gently for 30 mins until cabbage is tender.

Serves 4.

Baked Custard

Ingredients

1 whole egg or 2 egg yolks
1 tbsp sugar
300 ml milk
vanilla essence

Method

1 Beat the eggs and sugar, add the milk and essence. Pour into a greased pie dish.

2 Sprinkle the top with grated nutmeg. Bake in oven at 160°C, gas mark 3 in a water bath for 1 hour.

Minted Lemon Cup

Ingredients

250 ml water
75 g sugar
juice of 2 lemons, strained
1 tbsp chopped fresh mint leaves
1 large bottle soda water, chilled
2 kiwi fruit, peeled and sliced
ice cubes
4 pineapple cubes and mint sprigs to decorate

Method

1 Place water and sugar in a saucepan, stir over moderate heat until sugar dissolves, simmer for 2 mins. Remove and cool, mix with lemon juice and chopped mint.

2 At serving time, place lemon mixture in tall jugs and top up with an equal amount of soda water. Add kiwi slices and ice cubes, and decorate each serving with a pineapple cube and a sprig of mint.

Individuals grow at different rates and complete their growth at different ages.

With a suitable environment,

lack of illness,

and a good diet

The Healthy
Diet Pyramid

Eat Least
Sugar
Butter
Margarine   Oil

Eat Moderately
Milk
Cheese
Yoghurt
Lean Meat
Poultry Fish
Pulses Nuts
Eggs

Eat Most
Cereals
Bread
Vegetables
Fruit

the body will reach the peak of its growth.(Growth peak or potential is inherited from both parents).

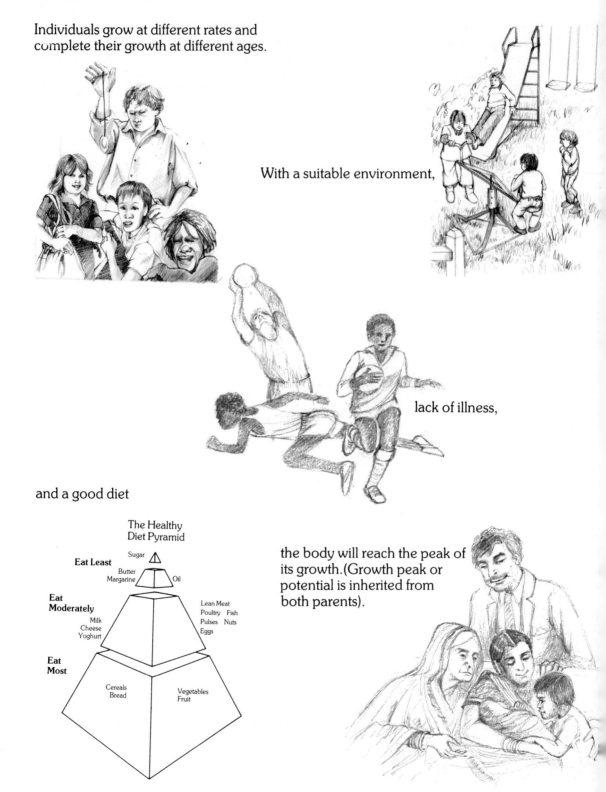

Individuals not only grow at different rates but they have different needs for nutrients as the various stages of the life cycle are experienced.

For the British diet, the daily kJ/kcal allowances expressed in the table below (in the left hand column) should, from the infant stage onwards, be made up of 30 per cent of kJ/kcal from fats, 11 per cent of kJ/kcal from proteins and the balance from carbohydrates.

Stage of development	Special dietary needs	
Pre-natal (foetus — 3rd – 9th month before birth)	During this very rapid period of growth the foetus receives nutrients from the mother who is only required to increase her energy intake by 1000 kJ/240 kcal per day during the last 6 months of the pregnancy (no increase needed in the first 3 months). This is the equivalent of a glass of milk and a slice of wholemeal bread or a piece of fruit. More protein, calcium, iron, vitamin C, folic acid, vitamin B_{12}, riboflavin, thiamin and nicotinic acid are required for the development of the foetus and the maintenance of the mother's tissues.	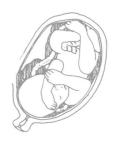
Post-natal (0–1 year) Recommended energy allowance months 483 kJ/115 kcal per kg body weight months – 1 year 420 kJ/100 kcal per kg body weight	The baby continues to grow rapidly for the first 6 to 9 months of its life. Preferably, babies are breast-fed for the first few months because breast milk has an accurate balance of nutrients for the growth of the baby. If it is necessary to bottle-feed the baby, care should be taken to make sure that the formula (milk mixture) used is suitable for that particular baby (health visitors and doctors help here). A variety of foods are introduced between five and six months of age, starting with baby cereal, then strained cooked vegetables and fruits, gradually taking in egg, bread, meat, cheese and whole cow's milk. By the age of 1 year, the baby can eat most family meals if cut very small and free of fat. If you compare food needs with body weight you will find that the need for all nutrients, but particularly protein, is great. That is, the amount of protein needed per kg of body weight is greater than for an adult. Look back at page 75 for the function of protein and reason why this is so.	
Infancy (1–3 years) Recommended energy allowance: year 5000 kJ/1200 kcal year 5750 kJ/1400 kcal	Growth is slower. Food needs differ little from those of a 1 year old. Each meal should contain a variety of foods which represent the proportions of the Healthy Diet Pyramid. Fat, salt and sugar should be kept to a minimum.	

Stage of development	Special dietary needs
Childhood (3–11 years)	Children are very active and are experiencing a very long, slow period of growth. The appetite may not be very large. Sugar, salt and fat should be kept low and the Healthy Diet Pyramid should be represented at each meal. In-between-meal snacks should be selected to be high in fibre, vitamins, minerals and carbohydrates, for example, fruit, bread and raw vegetables. Good eating habits developed during these years are frequently maintained later in life, as are poor eating habits.
Recommended energy allowance Girls 3–7: 7000 kJ/1680 kcal 7–11: 8500 kJ/2050 kcal Boys: 3–7: 7200 kJ/ 1725 kcal 7–11: 9500 kJ/ 2280 kcal	
Adolescence (11–17 years)	This is a high risk period for good nutrition. The reasons for this are: a more opportunity for unwise snacks b peer pressure — being influenced by how friends behave and how they eat c security — problems adjusting to rapid development and responsibilities d menstrual loss in girls can lead to iron deficiencies. Growth is very rapid, almost as rapid as before birth and babyhood.
Recommended energy allowance: Girls 12–14: 9000 kJ/2150 kcal, 15–17: 9000 kJ/2150 kcal Boys 12–14: 11000 kJ/2640 kcal, 15–17: 12000 kJ/2880 kcal	Sexual maturity occurs and the body proportions alter — girls' hips widen, boys' shoulders widen, height increases dramatically. Much more protein for cell synthesis and calcium for remodelling and growth of bones are needed, as are all the other hard and soft tissue nutrients. Some extra energy is needed for all this growth as the BMR rises, but remember that the demand for nutrients varies from one person to another, depending on just when particular stages of growth are being experienced. Nutritional needs can be compared with height during this period of the life cycle. Height, rather than body weight, is more significant in terms of need at this time. Adolescent females need 65 kJ/15 kcal per 1 cm of height. Adolescent males need 76 kJ/18 kcal per 1 cm of height. These figures are *only average* and the amount of physical activity will influence need. You could, however, *approximately* estimate your daily kJ/kcal need from these figures. All meals should be representative of the Healthy Diet Pyramid and the total diet should be planned to comply with the Dietary Guidelines. Snacking may be a very real problem as it is normal to feel hungry between meals if active and experiencing rapid growth. (See the Snack Guide on the next page.)

Snack Guide

Fat: Only 30% of our daily kJ/kcal intake should come from fat. For example, if our total daily kJ need = 9000 kJ/2150 kcal, then 2700 kJ/643 kcal can come from fat. In each 1 g of fat 37 kJ/9 kcal are available, therefore.

$\dfrac{2700}{37}$ = 73 g of pure fat is allowed

1 tbsp butter or margarine = 20 g fat (approximately)

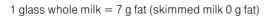

1 glass whole milk = 7 g fat (skimmed milk 0 g fat)

1 meat pie = 22 g fat

1 apple = 1 g fat

1 small hamburger or 1 doughnut or 1 Mars bar = 10 g fat

30 g potato crisps = 11 g fat

ice-cream in a cone or 1 chocolate biscuit = 5 g fat

Sodium: Common salt is sodium chloride and is our most common source of sodium. Our daily need of sodium = 200 mg.

25 g margarine = 200 mg

1 slice of bread = 130 mg

25 g roasted peanuts = 110 mg

1 small hamburger = 800 mg

1 meat pie = 600 mg

30 g potato crisps = 165 mg

1 orange or 1 pear or 1 apple = 2 mg

1 cup skimmed milk = 127 mg

Energy content of take-away foods:

medium hamburger + cheese = 1470 kJ/352 kcal

soft drink =
660 kJ/158 kcal

1 meat pie or ½ medium pizza = 2100 kJ/502 kcal

300 ml flavoured milk = 1080 kJ/258 kcal

average serving fish and chips = 2520 kJ/603 kcal

Stage of development	Special dietary needs
Adulthood (18–34 years) Recommended energy allowance Women: 9000 kJ/ 2150 kcal Men: 10150 kJ/ 2510 kcal	Growth is complete. Nutritional requirements are lower than that of the adolescent. Requirement depends very much on activity in employment and during sport, etc. Well balanced diets are essential, snacking should be avoided. As we have already learnt, what is adequate for one person might not be adequate for another. If the individual is healthy he/she should feel energetic, should not carry excess fat nor be excessively thin.
Middle Age (35–55 years) Recommended energy allowance Women: 9000 kJ/ 2150 kcal Men: 10000 kJ/ 2400 kcal	As the adult reaches the 'middle' years (around 45–55), he/she usually is less active and therefore requires less energy. The 'middle-aged spread' that some adults experience occurs because the dietary habits of past years are maintained as activity is reduced. This causes excess fat to be stored in the body. As activity reduces so must food intake. Obesity (being 20 per cent over the recommended weight for height, age and sex) is far too prevalent at this stage of the human life cycle. A healthy well-balanced diet must still be maintained. Between-meal snacks should be avoided. Diet-related diseases may become evident at this stage (heart disease, diabetes, blood pressure, obesity, diseases of the colon).

Stage of development	Special dietary needs
Elderly Women: 8000 kJ/ 1900 kcal Men: 10000 kJ/ 2400 kcal	The BMR and physical activity all reduce, therefore energy needs reduce. Protein, vitamin and mineral needs remain the same as they are in adulthood, therefore fat and carbohydrate intake should be reduced.
Special Groups The Athlete	There are no really different dietary requirements. A balanced, healthy diet and physical training make the athlete. Greater amounts of energy are needed because of the extra activity, but the proportions of the Healthy Diet Pyramid remain the same as for the non-athlete. Regimen (diet plan) for the athlete: a A balanced diet higher in energy than for an average person of the same age and sex. b Body weight maintained or slightly increased to allow for increased density of muscle tissue and/or to allow for natural increase due to growth if the athlete is a child or an adolescent. c A week or so before competing, reduce the carbohydrate intake and train very hard to use up the stores of glycogen (energy) in the muscles. d Change the diet abruptly 2–3 days before the event and eat a very high carbohydrate diet whilst tapering off training at the same time. This allows the muscles to store glycogen at about twice their normal level and will provide energy to last longer during an event.
The Vegetarian	There are 2 main types of vegetarians: 1 The lacto-ovo vegetarian who eats no meat but will eat animal foods such as eggs and dairy products. 2 The vegan who eats no animal products at all. Look back at page 75 for notes on high and low quality protein and the diagram on page 74 which shows how to improve the protein value of a meal. This will help you to understand how vegetarians manage their diet. The balance of amino acids is the most important consideration for this group. Vitamin B_{12} is a problem for the vegan as it is only found in animal foods. This vitamin must therefore be supplemented in their diets. To do this they can use Vitamin B_{12} fortified soya milk.
The Obese	When an individual is 20–25 per cent over the weight that is considered desirable for his/her height, age and sex, that individual is considered to be obese. 　Obesity is caused by taking in more food than is used up in energy. It does not necessarily mean that obese people eat more than non-obese people who perform the same activities, it means that they *need* less. They possibly have a lower BMR. An obese person is usually less energetic and being less energetic means kJ/kcal are not being burnt up—it is a kind of vicious circle. 　In an obese person the heart has to work very hard to pump the blood to these excessive layers of fat cells. This places extra strain on the heart and usually raises the blood pressure, causing a higher risk of heart problems. An obese person must *gradually* increase activity and reduce the normal food intake. Thus, more energy will be used up than taken in.

Stage of development	Special dietary needs

Acceptable weights as recommended by the Fogarty Conference, U.S.A. 1979 and the Royal College of Physicians, 1983

	MEN Weight without clothes (kg)			WOMEN Weight without clothes (kg)		
Height without shoes (m)	Accept-able average	Accept-able weight range	Obese	Accept-able average	Accept-able weight range	Obese
1.45				46.0	42–53	64
1.48				46.5	42–54	65
1.50				47.0	43–55	66
1.52				48.5	44–57	68
1.54				49.5	44–58	70
1.56				50.4	45–58	70
1.58	55.8	51–64	77	51.3	46–59	71
1.60	57.6	52–65	78	52.6	48–61	73
1.62	58.5	53–66	79	54.0	49–62	74
1.64	59.6	54–67	80	55.4	50–64	77
1.66	60.6	55–69	83	56.8	51–65	78
1.68	61.7	56–71	85	58.1	52–66	79
1.70	63.5	58–73	88	60.0	53–67	80
1.72	65.0	59–74	89	61.3	55–69	83
1.74	66.5	60–75	90	62.6	56–70	84
1.76	68.0	62–77	92	64.0	58–72	86
1.78	69.4	64–79	95	65.3	59–74	89
1.80	71.0	65–80	96			
1.82	72.6	66–82	98			
1.84	74.2	67–84	101			
1.86	75.8	69–86	103			
1.88	77.6	71–88	106			
1.90	79.3	73–90	108			
1.92	81.0	75–93	112			
BMI*	22.0	20.1–25.0	30.0	20.8	18.7–23.8	28.6*

*Body mass index = weight in kg/height^2 in metres
(Note: Tables are not useful for children as they are growing.)

Body Mass Index (BMI)
This is one way which can indicate whether a person's weight is desirable or whether they are overweight or obese. The index is calculated by dividing the weight, measured in kilograms, by the height squared, measured in metres.

For example a person weighing 58 kg with a height of 1.66 metres would have a BMI of

$$BMI = \frac{wt(kg)}{ht^2(m)} = \frac{58}{1.6^2} = \frac{58}{2.56} = 22.7$$

A desirable score is between 20–25. Above 25 indicates someone who is overweight.

Stage of development	Special dietary needs

'Crash' diets are fads, they do not last. It is best for the obese person to:

- cut out food eaten between meals and maintain 'normal' meals (not increase them to make up for omitted snacks).
- remove any foods with added sugar from meals
- make sure all fat is trimmed from meat, skin is removed from chicken and no foods are fried.
- ensure that the *eat most* and *eat moderately* foods are in proportion— the *eat least* foods can be deleted if this is done.
- not to be in a rush to lose the weight, and to remember how long it took to put the weight on! The *gradually modified* reducing diet (that is, not radically different diet) is the one that is likely to be successful. The obese person should not become fanatical and influenced by advertisements that emphasise slimness and beauty—the people in advertisements are artificial, hopefully the obese person is not!

Workshop

1 Interview a physical education teacher or a sporting coach to find out what he/she thinks about the diet of the athlete. Interviewing people is an important method of research. Plan your questions first.

2 Calculate your Body Mass Index. What does it tell you about your weight?

3 Plan a daily diet for:
   a a lacto-ovo vegetarian,
   b a vegan.

4 Look back at page 4 which shows a decision-making flow chart. Use this flow chart as a basis to construct a flow chart for yourself showing how you decide what to have for lunch.

5 This section, 'How Much Food Do I Need', is written in three parts:
   - Energy,
   - Proportion,
   - The Human Life Cycle.
   Write a paragraph which draws information from each of these three parts and describes what influences how much food *you* need.

6 Conduct a survey using one of the school's sports teams as your sample. (To revise how to conduct a survey, see Introduction). Ask each team member to write down everything they eat for one day (food and amount), compare each team member's diet with the Healthy Diet Pyramid, then compile all data and compare with the Pyramids. Discuss your results. Keeping all data confidential (that is, do not reveal the names of the subjects), report back to the team on how many team members need to improve their diet and on the average

adequacy of the diet of the team. Instruct the team on how they might improve their diet. Write up this research as a practical exercise with an aim, procedure, data presentation, discussion, conclusion and recommendations. This whole activity will, of course, be done under the close supervision of your teacher.

7   Research the different types of commercially produced baby formulas available. Assess the information on the label for readability (that is, how easy is it to understand) and compare the products for nutritional value according to the label.

8   Look back at page 92 and the table on the adolescent's special dietary needs. In the left hand column you will notice that the recommended daily amounts of kJ kcal are quite different for girls and boys. What is the main reason for the difference in the fifteen to eighteen year olds? Why has the girls' allowance dropped and the boys' increased?

9   **Thirty-seven Diet Words**
Find the thirty-seven diet words and write a paragraph about your health as it relates to diet using at least twenty of the words in the puzzle.

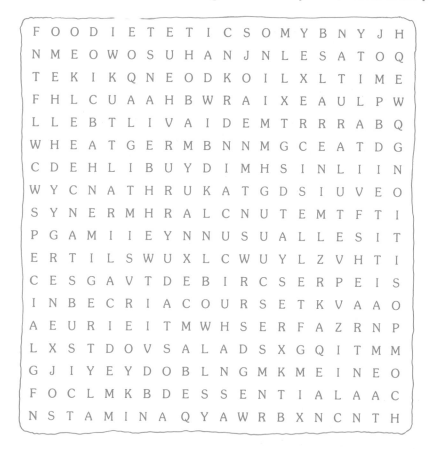

```
F O O D I E T E T I C S O M Y B N Y J H
N M E O W O S U H A N J N L E S A T O Q
T E K I K Q N E O D K O I L X L T I M E
F H L C U A A H B W R A I X E A U L P W
L L E B T L I V A I D E M T R R R A B Q
W H E A T G E R M B N N M G C E A T D G
C D E H L I B U Y D I M H S I N L I I N
W Y C N A T H R U K A T G D S I U V E O
S Y N E R M H R A L C N U T E M T F T I
P G A M I I E Y N N U S U A L L E S I T
E R T I L S W U X L C W U Y L Z V H T I
C E S G A V T D E B I R C S E R P E I S
I N B E C R I A C O U R S E T K V A A O
A E U R I E I T M W H S E R F A Z R N P
L X S T D O V S A L A D S X G Q I T M M
G J I Y E Y D O B L N G M K M E I N E O
F O C L M K B D E S S E N T I A L A A C
N S T A M I N A Q Y A W R B X N C N T H
```

10   Try some of the low sodium and low fat recipes that follow Investigation No. 16.

Investigation No. 16
The Acceptability of Food

Aim

- To discover the acceptability of vegetable protein products as an alternative protein source

Procedure

a The teacher will prepare a number of samples and set them out in groups identified by numbers only, for example,

Group A:	1	Topside stew
	2	Topside stew/TVP mixture (50–50)
	3	TVP stew
Group B:	4	Vegetarian sausages
	5	Beef sausages
Group C:	6	Meat loaf
	7	Soya loaf
Group D:	8	Homogenised cow's milk
	9	Skimmed cow's milk
	10	Soya milk
Group E:	11	Wheat flour biscuits
	12	Soya flour biscuits

b Pupils examine each sample for appearance, odour and flavour, filling in a table like the one following for each food. Pupils should tick their responses as they are examining. After the whole class is finished, scores for each column should be added and entered, then added across for the total score.

Sample no		Excellent (9)	Very good (8)	Good (7)	Satisfactory (6)	Average (5)	Fair (4)	Poor (3)	Very poor (2)	Unacceptable (1)	Total score from class
1	Name: (filled in after sampling) Appearance Odour Taste										
2	Name: Appearance Odour Taste										

Sample no		Excellent (9)	Very good (8)	Good (7)	Satisfactory (6)	Average (5)	Fair (4)	Poor (3)	Very poor (2)	Unacceptable (1)	Total score from class
3	Name: Appearance Odour Taste										
4	Name: Appearance Odour Taste										
5	Name: Appearance Odour Taste										
6	Name: Appearance Odour Taste										
7	Name: Appearance Odour Taste										
8	Name: Appearance Odour Taste										

c Following completion of the scoring, the names of the samples will be revealed and entered on the sheet.

d The foods with the highest scores are to be seen as the most acceptable. Discuss the results as a class. Compare all the scores of the vegetable protein foods with those of the animal proteins. Which were the most acceptable?

e Find out some possible variables existing in your classroom:
— How many people are vegetarians?
— How many people regularly eat the vegetable protein foods sampled?
— How might these statistics have influenced your results?

Recipes to Try

Chicken and Orange Kebabs

Ingredients

2 oranges
300 g cooked chicken
280 g mushrooms
200 ml low fat yoghurt
60 ml orange juice
½ tsp grated orange rind
few shakes pepper
½ lettuce, washed
chopped parsley for garnish

Method

1 Peel oranges, remove pith and cut flesh into bite-size segments.

2 Remove skin of chicken and cut the chicken into 2.5 cm cubes.

3 Thread skewers alternately with orange pieces, mushrooms and chicken until all pieces are used.

4 Combine yoghurt, orange rind and orange juice and season with pepper.

5 Arrange kebabs on a bed of fresh lettuce leaves and top with orange dressing. Garnish with chopped parsley.
Serves 4.

Chinese Leek Soup

Ingredients

100 g thinly sliced onion
35 g sliced celery
1 tbsp soy sauce
few shakes pepper
750 ml water
150 g sliced leek plus green tops
1 clove garlic, crushed

Method

1 Place all ingredients in saucepan and simmer for 45 mins.
Serves 4

Lemon Plaice

Ingredients

4 plaice fillets
2 bay leaves
125 ml lemon juice
pepper to taste
1 can asparagus spears
½ tsp paprika

Method

1 Arrange fish in a shallow casserole, add bay leaves and pour over lemon juice, sprinkle with pepper.

2 Cover fish completely with drained asparagus spears and sprinkle with paprika.

3 Cover and cook in a moderate oven for 20–25 mins or until fish is just cooked.
Serves 4.

Cinnamon Baked Banana

Ingredients

4 medium bananas
60 ml low calorie lemon soft drink
juice of one lemon
1 tsp cinnamon
½ tsp nutmeg

Method

1 Thinly slice bananas and place in layers in a small, flat casserole. Sprinkle spices over bananas.

2 Mix juice and soft drink and pour over. Bake 20 mins in a moderate oven.
Serves 4.

Lentil Rissoles

Ingredients

125 g lentils
1 finely chopped onion
2 potatoes, cooked and mashed
100 g breadcrumbs
50 g finely chopped almonds
25 g sesame seeds
¼ tsp salt
2 tbsp parsley, chopped
1 egg

Method

1 Soak lentils for 5 mins in warm water.

2 Drain lentils, cover with plenty of fresh water and boil for 20 mins until tender, drain and purée through a sieve or in a blender.

3 Add onion, potato, breadcrumbs, nuts, sesame seeds, salt, parsley and egg. Mix well.

4 Shape into 12 rissoles.

5 Place on greased tray in moderate oven (190°C, gas mark 5) for 25–30 mins.

6 Serve hot with salad.
Serves 6.

Part 3

Finding Out About Food

5 About Food

Food Facts and Fallacies

Many people are misinformed about food. Many people are difficult to convince of the facts about food.

To help you to answer questions you might have, or, for you to be able to enter intelligently into discussions amongst friends and relatives, a collection of common *fallacies* (what is incorrectly believed) and *facts* (what is the truth) makes up this chapter. You will most likely come up with other fallacies and will be able to discover the facts from class discussions and research.

Fallacy
Butter is more fattening than margarine.
Fact
Butter and margarine each contain 3040 kJ (730 kcal) per 100 g. In fact margarine contains as much sodium, less vitamin A and about the same B vitamins as butter.

Fallacy
Brown sugar is better than white sugar.
Fact
White sugar is almost 100 per cent carbohydrate. Brown sugar contains traces of minerals but such tiny amounts that they make no difference to the diet.

Fallacy
Honey is a 'natural' food, good for health and non-fattening.
Fact
Honey is approximately 80 per cent carbohydrate. All sugars essentially come from natural sources. There is no scientific evidence that honey has any particular health giving properties. Because of its high carbohydrate content, honey, like other sugars, should be avoided by anyone on a low energy diet. Because of its viscosity, honey clings to the teeth surfaces for longer than crystalline sugars. The energy value of honey is almost as high as sugar (16 kJ/4 kcal per gram). There are small amounts of other nutrients in honey but because of the small quantities eaten they are insignificant and it is easier to obtain them from other foods, for example, it would take 5 tablespoons of honey to yield the amount of iron in 30 g meat.

Fallacy
Organically grown vegetables are the most nutritious.
Fact
There is no scientific evidence to support this claim. Organically grown foods have exactly the same nutritional value as those grown with fertilisers and there is no proof that fertilisers are harmful. Organically grown vegetables are more expensive. Vegetables straight from your own garden are the most nutritious. Those from the greengrocer and the deep freeze can deteriorate if they are kept too long, although they are good quality when fresh. Growing your own bean sprouts, such as alfalfa, mung bean and lentils, provides fresh crisp vegetables which also contain B vitamins, iron and vitamin C.

Fallacy
Yoghurt is a wonder food which prolongs life and beauty.
Fact
Yoghurt is a good source of nutrients but the other claims are incorrect. Yoghurt is made by adding a bacterial culture to milk. It is rich in protein, calcium and riboflavin, as is milk. There is no truth that the added bacteria

overcome harmful bacteria in the large intestine. Intestinal bacteria are necessary for the synthesis of several vitamins, it is wrong to believe they are harmful. Yoghurt has no effect on them unless you eat enormous amounts.

Fallacy

Polyunsaturated oil is less fattening than saturated fats and contains more vitamins.

Fact

Pure fat always has the same energy content 37 kJ/g, 9 kcal/g. All oils, lard and dripping are pure fat. Butter and margarine are about 85% fat—the rest is water, so they have slightly less energy.

Fallacy

Adults do not need milk in their diet. Milk and cheese cause constipation.

Fact

Milk contains protein, calcium and B vitamins in good quantities, While these nutrients are necessary throughout life, children particularly need calcium. It is difficult to obtain enough calcium if milk or milk products are not included in the diet. No food in itself causes constipation; it is frequently caused by a lack of fibre in the diet.

Fallacy

'Health' bars are a good substitute for lollies.

Fact

'Health' bars made from glucose, honey or dried fruits are usually very expensive and have only marginal, if any, advantages over ice lollies. The very sticky texture of many of these bars encourages them to become stuck between the teeth. Fruit and nuts are a better substitute.

Fallacy

Toast contains less energy than bread.

Fact

A slice of bread loses moisture and becomes lighter when toasted, so gram-for-gram toast has fewer kilojoules, but slice for slice, they are the same.

Fallacy

During pregnancy the mother should eat for two.

Fact

During the first 3 months of pregnancy dietary needs do not alter. During the last 6 months dietary needs only increase by 1000 kJ per day (250 kcal). The mother's body becomes much more efficient at using the nutrients taken in; obesity must be avoided during pregnancy. (See page 91).

Fallacy

Starchy foods such as bread, cereals and potatoes are 'fattening' and cannot be included in a weight reducing diet.

Fact

Bread, cereals and potatoes are all relatively cheap and contain valuable amounts of protein, fibre, vitamins and minerals. As long as they are not eaten to excess and butter, cream and rich gravy are kept to a minimum, these foods should form a large part of *all* diets.

Fallacy

Grapefruit is a good slimming food because it helps to burn up fat.

Fact

No foods should be described as 'slimming' foods. No foods burn up fat. Fat in the body can either remain stored or can be burnt up for energy. It will only be burnt up if the body activity needs more energy than is provided in the daily food intake. Grapefruit is low in energy and may be included in a slimming diet.

Fallacy

Exercising is better than dieting for losing weight.

Fact

A programme to lose weight must involve dietary change plus a gradual increase in exercise (see page 95 for notes on obesity).

Fallacy

A high protein diet is necessary for anyone engaging in excessive exercise.

Fact

A normal balanced diet is what is required, slightly higher in energy than one for an average person of the same age and sex (see page 95 for notes on the athlete).

Fallacy

Foods sold in 'health' food shops are good for you.

Fact

It is wrong to think that because a food is sold by a 'health' food shop it is automatically good for you. Dried fruit, for example, is high in fibre but it is so rich in sugar that it would be bad in large quantities for a person on a slimming diet. Many goods bought in a 'health' food shop can be bought more cheaply at supermarkets.

Fallacy

It is wise to take vitamin supplements (tablets) as the more vitamins you take the healthier you will be.

Fact

The body can only absorb as much as it needs of vitamins. It can store the fat-soluble vitamins A, D, E and K. Any excess of the water-soluble vitamins B and C is excreted in the urine. If you are eating properly, vitamin supplements are unnecessary.

Fallacy

Breakfast is not an important meal.

Fact

Studies have shown that those who skip breakfast do not work and think as well in the late hours of the morning as those who eat breakfast. It has also been shown that in many cases a mid-morning snack cannot be considered a satisfactory substitute for breakfast.

Fallacy

Fat babies are healthy babies.

Fact

Fatness at any time of life is not healthy. Fat babies frequently become fat adults.

Where Does Food Come From?

Food is the name for all the different things we eat and drink to keep us alive. Food makes us grow, gives us energy and keeps us healthy if we have the right amounts of the right foods. The plants and animals we eat are grown on farms, in orchards and in market gardens. We also eat food from the sea.

In Britain, we have large quantities and varieties of meat to choose from: beef cattle, sheep, pigs, rabbits, chicken and fish. Some animals give us a lot of different foods, for example, cattle give us meat and milk. Milk is processed so that it is available in many different forms and is used to extract cream and make butter, cheese and yoghurt.

The plants we eat are many and varied. Our main cereal crop is wheat. Some plants are grown in Britain—potatoes in Jersey and Cheshire, raspberries in Scotland, plums in Worcestershire, apples in Kent. Others are imported from Europe and the rest of the world: tomatoes from Holland, pineapples from the West Indies.

Some food is processed after it is taken from the growing areas. It is taken to factories and processed to give us a greater variety of food that we can keep in cans and packets for long periods of time. Wheat, for example, is processed into flour and made into bread, spaghetti, breakfast cereals and many other foods.

Workshop

1 a List all the different forms of cow's milk that we can buy.
  b Do we only use milk from cows?

c If you answered *no* to 'b', name the other animal(s) we use as a
source of milk.

2 a Choose any two of the animals that give us meat (*see* list above). For
your two selected animals list all the different foods we use from
those animals.

b Do the animals you have chosen give us anything useful other than
food?

3 The map below shows the main wheat growing areas of the world.
a What kind of climate do you think is the best for growing wheat?
b Wheat is a cereal. It is an edible seed or grain. Can you list *five* other
cereal crops?
c Mark on the map of the world areas where the five cereal crops are
grown (you should use reference books for this).

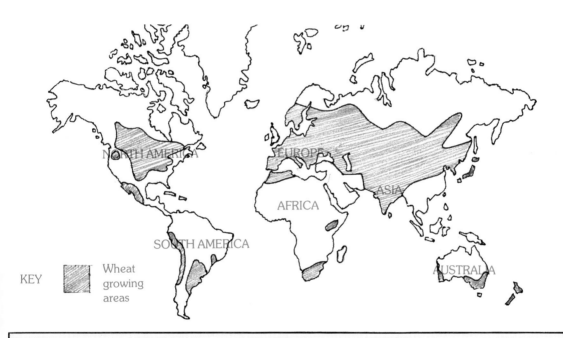

KEY — Wheat growing areas

Investigation No. 17
Food Origins

Aim

To understand where food comes from.

Procedure

a Divide into groups of four.

b Read through the recipes at the end of this exercise, or those selected by your teacher.

c Divide the workload evenly between the members of your group.

d Collect the ingredients, examining any packaging as you do so. Prepare the menu.

e Serve and eat the meal. Clean up the Home Economics Room according to the procedure learnt in class.

f In the table below, all the ingredients you used are listed in the left hand column. Fill in the three other columns correctly. One example has been completed for you as a guide.

Food used	Processed (yes/no)	Origin	Where grown
chop	no	lamb	farm
tomato			
butter			
bacon			
onion			
parsley			
breadcrumbs			
salt			
pepper			
cheese			
apple			
milk			
custard powder			
sugar			

Menu

Grilled Lamb Chops
Hot Stuffed Tomatoes
Stewed Apple
Custard

Recipes to Try

Grilled Lamb Chops

Ingredients

4 lamb loin chops
4 cocktail sticks
4 small sprigs of parsley

Method

1 Light the grill.

2 Trim any excess fat from the chops, leaving at least 1 cm thickness.

3 Roll the 'tail' of the chop neatly, securing with a cocktail stick.

4 Place the chops under the preheated grill.

5 Turn the chops after 5 mins — use tongs.

6 Grill 5 mins on the other side then turn the chop again. Repeat until the chops are cooked to the taste of the diner. However, they should not be burnt.

7 Remove from the grill, remove cocktail sticks and serve on a warm plate.

Serves 4.

Hot Stuffed Tomatoes

Ingredients

4 even-sized tomatoes
2 tsp oil
½ bacon rasher
¼ chopped onion (2 tsp)
1 tsp chopped parsley
2 tbsp fresh breadcrumbs
2 shakes pepper
2 tbsp grated cheese

Method

1 Cut a small slice from each tomato at the end opposite the stalk.

2 Scoop out the centres of the tomatoes.

3 Remove rind from bacon and cut the bacon into 1 cm squares.

4 Heat oil in a pan, add the bacon and onion. Fry for 5 mins.

5 Add parsley, breadcrumbs and all other ingredients. Mix evenly.

6 Remove from heat and fill the tomatoes with the mixture.

7 Place on a tray and bake in the oven at 200°C, gas mark 6 for 15 mins.

8 Serve hot.

Serves 4.

Stewed Apple

Ingredients

2 large cooking apples
1 tbsp sugar
100 ml water
1 clove

Method

1 Peel, core and slice apples.

2 Place all ingredients in saucepan and simmer for about 10 mins or until glassy. Remove clove.

Serves 4.

Custard

Ingredients

300 ml milk
1 tbsp custard powder
2 tsp sugar

Method

1 Place custard powder in small bowl and blend with a little milk.

2 Place blended custard and all other ingredients into a small saucepan on medium–low heat.

3 Stir mixture constantly until thickened.

Serves 4.

Fresh Vegetable Facts

Item and availability	What to look for	Nutrition and energy	Storage	Method of cooking
Aubergine All year. Cheapest in summer.	Dark purple to purple black colour with glossy skin. Firm to touch.	High water content. Small amounts of most minerals and vitamins. Some fibre 105 kJ/100 g.	Keep for about 7 days in refrigerator crisper.	Bake, boil fry or mash.

4.2 kJ = 1 kcal

Fresh Vegetable Facts

Item and availability	What to look for	Nutrition and energy	Storage	Method of cooking
Brussels sprouts Available August–May.	Bright green, firm leaves.	Very good source of vitamin C. 75 kJ/100 g when cooked.	Wrap in vented plastic and store in a cool place. Use within 5 days.	Cut a cross in the stem end and boil or steam.
Cabbage All year. Cheapest in summer	Firm heads. Outer leaves should be strongly coloured and not limp.	Good source of vitamin C. Some calcium and fibre. 66 kJ/100 g boiled.	Trim lightly and remove outer leaves. Wrap in plastic and store in a cool place. Use within a week of purchase.	May be boiled, steamed or stir-fried.
Carrots All year. Cheapest in autumn.	Firm, smooth and well formed. Deep orange to red in colour.	Outstanding source of vitamin A, good source of fibre. 79 kJ/100 g boiled.	Store in a plastic bag in a cool place.	Steam, boil, braise or shred. Delicious raw or cooked.
Cauliflower All year. Cheapest in summer.	Should not have a ricey appearance or obvious flowers. Look for firm white compact heads without spots or bruises.	Very good source of vitamin C, fair source of folic acid and fibre. 40 kJ/100 g boiled.	Store in plastic bag in a cool place. Use before heads turn brown.	Steam or boil and top with cheese sauce. Use raw in salads and soup.
Lettuce All year. Cheapest in summer.	Choose firm green heads with crisp, blemish-free leaves.	Some potassium, fibre and folic acid. 51 kJ/100 g raw.	Perishable. Store in plastic in refrigerator crisper and use as soon as possible.	Usually eaten fresh. May be braised, stir fried or added to soup.
Mushrooms All year.	Look for firmness, white or creamy colour and unbroken shape. Avoid withered mushrooms.	Good source of nicotinic acid and riboflavin. Excellent source of potassium. 53 kJ/100 g raw, 863 kJ/100 g fried.	Perishable. Store in paper bag in refrigerator. Use within 2–3 days.	Can be eaten raw, microwaved or sautéed in butter. Cook only lightly.
Onions All year. Cheapest in autumn.	Firm, with clear outer skin, no dark patches or signs of sprouting.	Small amount of vitamins and minerals. Rich in sugars. 99 kJ/100 g raw, 1424 kJ/100 g fried.	Store in cool, dry and dark area.	Sauté, boil, bake, cream or fry.
Peas Available only in summer.	Pods should be bright green in colour. Very firm and full pods indicate over-maturity.	Some protein and iron. Fair source of thiamin and folic acid. Good source of dietary fibre. 223 kJ/100 g boiled.	Store in plastic bag in refrigerator. Use as soon as possible.	Boil, steam, or braise with lettuce.

4.2 kJ = 1 kcal

Fresh Vegetable Facts

Item and availability	What to look for	Nutrition and energy	Storage	Method of cooking
Pepper All year. Cheapest in summer.	Well-shaped, thick walled and firm, with a uniform glossy colour (deep red or bright green).	Very good source of vitamin C. Fair source of vitamin A. 65 kJ/100 g raw.	Store in plastic bag in a cool place. Use within 5 days.	Delicious raw in salads. May be stuffed and baked or used in soups and casseroles.
Potatoes All year. Cheapest in autumn.	Firm and unbroken skin with no green tinge. There should be no dark spots or green shoots.	Fairly good source of vitamin C. Good source of potassium and dietary fibre. Some protein. 343 kJ/100 g boiled, 1065 kJ/100 g chips.	Store in a cool, dry and dark area. Do not store in refrigerator.	Bake, boil, fry, steam or mash.
Runner beans Summer	Firm, long straight pods, crisp enough to snap. Good green colour.	Small mineral and vitamin content particularly vitamin C. Some fibre. 83 kJ/100 g when cooked.	Wash, drain and store in vented plastic bag in a cool place. Use soon after purchase.	Steam, boil or microwave. May be lightly tossed in butter to glaze. Do not overcook.
Sweet Corn All year. Cheapest September–October.	Husks fresh and green in colour. Kernels well filled, tender, milky, and pale yellow in colour.	Some protein and vitamin A. Good source of dietary fibre. 520 kJ/100 g boiled.	Wrap in vented plastic bag and keep refrigerated.	Boil, bake or steam.
Tomatoes All year. Cheapest in summer.	Free of blemish. Firmly fleshed, and weight heavy in the hand.	Good source of vitamin C, some vitamin A. 60 g kJ/100 g raw.	Only refrigerate when over-ripe. Always remove from refrigerator 1 hour before eating to improve flavour.	Use fresh or stew; bake, sauté, stuff, or prepare as a sauce.

4.2 kJ = 1 kcal

The Potato

To discover more about the versatility of vegetables we will look more closely at the potato which is probably *the* most consumed vegetable in the world. The potato is a *tuber*. Tubers are underground stems swollen with food. Food made in the leaves of the plant passes to the end of the roots in the ground. These swell and form potatoes. The 'eyes' on potatoes are tiny leaves and buds each of which can produce a new plant the following year.

Varieties

'New' potatoes have a rather waxy flesh and thin skin. They are not fully matured tubers and they do not keep well. 'Old' potatoes have a firm skin and a more floury, juicy texture. 'New' potatoes are best just boiled and served hot or cold in a salad. They are not easily digested so should not be given to babies, very old people or sick people.

'Old' potatoes are more flexible for cooking methods and are easily digested when boiled, steamed or baked in their skin. When fried or roasted they absorb quite a lot of the cooking fat or oil. They keep well if stored in a cool dark place.

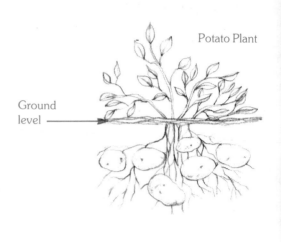

Potato Plant

Ground level

Nutritive Value

The potato is a very good food. It is high in fibre and starch, and is the major source of vitamin C in the British diet. A potato itself is less fattening than bread, rice and spaghetti but it should not be covered in gravy, butter or grated cheese.

Cooking potatoes

When potatoes are peeled they are affected by oxygen in the air which turns them brown, they should therefore be covered with water until ready to cook. But do not leave them soaking too long as this encourages vitamin and mineral loss which,

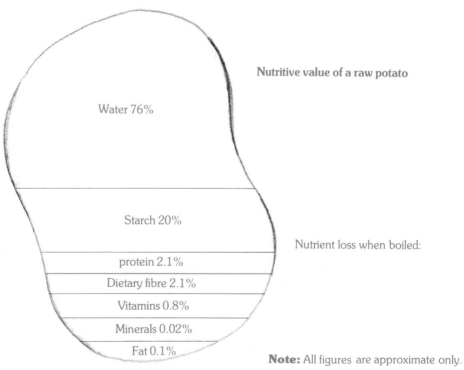

Water 76%

Starch 20%

protein 2.1%

Dietary fibre 2.1%

Vitamins 0.8%

Minerals 0.02%

Fat 0.1%

Nutritive value of a raw potato

Nutrient loss when boiled:

Note: All figures are approximate only.

s you can see from the diagram opposite, is
lready considerable. Whenever possible,
:ave the skin on potatoes, or if you must
:eel them do so very thinly. (The greatest
:oncentration of vitamins and minerals is
1st under the skin.)

Recipes to Try

Pommes Anna

The French for potato is *pomme de terre*. When
1sing this on a menu it is shortened to just *pomme*)

1gredients

potatoes
tbsp melted margarine

1ethod

Peel potatoes and trim to a cylindrical shape.
Slice into thin rounds.
Grease 4 dariole moulds with margarine and brush
each slice of potato with margarine as you arrange
the potato slices neatly into the mould.
Bake in a hot oven 45–55 mins until tender.
Turn out and sprinkle with chopped parsley.

Deep Fried Potatoes

1l the following potato preparations are to be deep
ied. When they are cut to the desired shape, soak
1em briefly in a bowl of salt water. Drain and *dry
1oroughly* then lower gently into hot oil.

Pommes Bataille

1tatoes are peeled and washed then cut into 1½ cm
ce.

Pommes Copeaux

Potatoes are peeled, washed and cut into 1 cm slices.
Each slice is then cut into a round with a scone
cutter — as large as will fit on the potato. Using a
vegetable peeler, go around and around each slice,
thus producing long ribbons. Take care when drying
that you do not break them too much.

Pommes Pailles

Peel and wash potatoes. Square the ends and cut into
3 mm slices. Holding two or three slices together slice
through in 3 mm slices again, thus producing straws.

Pommes Frites

Peel and wash potatoes and trim to a reasonably neat
square or rectangle. Cut into lengths 1 cm square on
the end.

Pommes Duchesse
Ingredients

3 or 4 potatoes (or all the scraps from trimming other
potato dishes to shape)
1 tbsp margarine
1 egg yolk
pinch of nutmeg

Method

1 Peel and wash potatoes and cut to medium-sized pieces.

2 Cook in a steamer until tender — about 20–25 mins depending on the size of the pieces. (Steaming retains more vitamins than boiling).

3 Mash the potatoes with the other ingredients.

4 Using two forks, pile eggcup-sized portions on a greased baking tray. Roughen the sides of the piles decoratively with the forks.

5 Brown in a hot oven.

Pommes Marquise

Using the Pommes Duchesse mixture above, pipe nests of potato about 6 cm in diameter and 3 cm high on the sides on to a lightly greased tray. Fill the centres with peeled diced tomato, sprinkle with a few drops of melted butter and place under the grill until just coloured.

Scalloped Potatoes

Ingredients

350 g potatoes
salt and pepper
1 tbsp flour
250 ml milk
1 tbsp margarine

Method

1 Peel and wash potatoes and cut into thin slices.

2 Place potato in casserole, sprinkling each layer with flour, salt and pepper and margarine.

3 Heat milk.

4 Pour milk over potato, cover casserole.

5 Bake for about 50–60 mins at 190°C, gas mark 5.
Serves 4.

Jacket Potato

Ingredients

1 potato
1 tsp plain yoghurt or sour cream
½ finely chopped spring onion

Method

1 Scrub potato until quite clean.

2 Make 3 or 4 holes with a skewer.

3 Place on oven bars in an oven on 200°C, gas mark for 1 hour or until a skewer will pass through easily, or the potato can be microwaved on full power for about 6 minutes, turning once.

4 Cut a cross in top of potato and squeeze open. Fill with yoghurt and garnish with onion.
Serves 1.

Pommes Gratinées

Proceed as for **Jacket potato** recipe until step 3 is completed.
Cut a slice from the top of the potato and scoop out t flesh. Purée and mix with a little butter. Fill back into shell and sprinkle with cheese, grill until golden.

Stuffed Baked Potatoes

Baked potatoes can be stuffed with just about anything from cottage cheese to caviar. Choose larg potatoes and bake in the oven until tender (see above). Cut in half and scoop out insides. Mix with chosen ingredients and pile back into potato shells. Reheat in hot oven or under the grill.

Suggested fillings

1 Cream cheese, black pepper and parsley.
2 Chicken, sour cream and chives.
3 Chicken, ham, mushrooms and mayonnaise.
4 Bacon, mushrooms, chopped herbs and garlic.
5 Grated cheese, egg yolk and mustard.
6 Fillet of white fish, mornay sauce, grated cheese and parsley.

Potatoes à la Provençale

Ingredients

450 g baby new potatoes
25 g margarine
3 tbsp olive oil
3 cloves garlic
juice from 1 lemon
chopped parsley
salt and pepper
grated nutmeg

Method

Melt margarine and oil in a heavy pan and add the potatoes, garlic and a pinch of nutmeg. Heat very gently until tender.

Before serving season with salt and pepper, add the lemon juice and sprinkle with parsley

Serves 4.

Potato Gnocchi

An Italian dish normally eaten as a first course with Parmesan cheese or tomato sauce.

Ingredients

500 g potatoes
100 g plain flour
1 tbsp margarine
salt and black pepper
1 egg beaten
Parmesan cheese

Method

1 Peel and boil potatoes. Drain and sieve to make a puree, keeping them as dry as possible.

2 Mix in flour, margarine and egg. Season with salt and pepper and knead into a dough.

3 Make into gnocchi by rolling into thickness of a finger and cutting into pieces about 3 cm long. Press each one round your finger to make a crescent shape then drop into a pan of boiling salted water. Cook for about 3 mins until they rise to the surface then remove with a slotted spoon. Keep hot, sprinkling with Parmesan cheese. Pour over melted butter and serve with cheese or tomato sauce.

Serves 3–4.

Potato Pancakes

Ingredients

350 g grated raw potato
1 small grated onion
1 tbsp flour
1 egg
salt and black pepper
oil for cooking

Method

1 Mix potato, onion and seasoning. Blend in the egg and flour.

2 Shape into smallish flat cakes and shallow fry in hot oil until golden, turning once.

3 Drain well on kitchen paper before serving. Add chopped bacon, herbs or garlic to the mixture for variation.

Serves 4.

Workshop

1 Rate each of the potato recipes you tried. Copy the scale below into your book and put a tick in one of the boxes.

Recipe name:...........

Very Good   Poor

Write in your book your reasons for each rating.

2 **Vegetable Crossword**
Clues

Across

1 Potatoes are packed in one to take them to market.
3 Vegetables that are not stored correctly will ... and be unsuitable to eat.
5 Most vegetables are served this way in salads.
7 A cooking utensil.
8 A very long vegetable, grows on a vine.
12 Many vegetables that grow above the ground are .....
14 The ... of vegetable cookery is to retain as many nutrients as possible.
15 Round and green.
16 Vegetables are boiled in this.
17 A little like lettuce with curly leaves.
18 The nationality of a famous tennis player as well as a vegetable.
19 Makes you cry.

Down

1 Deep red root, usually pickled.
2 A type of sweet potato.
3 Lettuce is usually served ...
4 Some form of dressing is usually served ... salad
6 New potatoes have flesh of this texture.
7 A very popular tuber, which can be served in many different ways.
9 Cinderella's coach!
10 Can be green, purple or yellow.
11 Looks like a carrot that had a fright.
12 Relatives of onions and national vegetable of Wales.
13 If vegetables are cooked this way it increases their fat content.
16 Vegetables that are ... should not be put into hot fat.

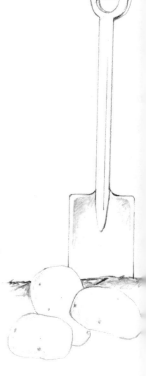

3 Only a few vegetables are listed in *Fresh Vegetable Facts* (p. 109–111). Consult your local greengrocer and the library to find out availability, what to look for, nutrition and energy, storage and methods of cooking for these vegetables: beetroot, courgettes, leeks, marrow, okra, parsnips, plaintain, spinach, swede, sweet potato, turnip, yam.

4 Prepare a buffet of vegetables from the following vegetable recipes.

Rate all your results as shown in activity 1. To do this, taste at least six of the prepared dishes.

Recipes To Try

Italian Vegetable Soup

Ingredients

2 tsp oil
1 medium carrot, thinly sliced
1 leek, washed and thinly sliced
1 small white turnip, peeled and diced
1 clove garlic, crushed
800 ml beef stock (made with stock cube)
415 g can red kidney beans, drained
½ tsp tomato paste
1 sprig parsley, chopped
black pepper
pinch dried thyme

Method

1 In a large saucepan, heat oil and add carrot, leek, celery, turnip and garlic.

2 Cover pan and fry gently for 5 minutes, shaking pan frequently.

3 Pour off excess oil, add stock and bring to boiling point.

4 Stir in beans, tomato paste, parsley, pepper and thyme. Cover and simmer for 30–40 minutes.

Serves 4

Chinese Vegetables

Ingredients

1 small aubergine
125 g Brussels sprouts (optional)
2 medium-sized carrots
1 small red pepper
1 small green pepper
½ cucumber (optional)
3 sticks celery
100 g fresh bean sprouts
1 clove garlic, crushed
200 ml chicken stock
1 tsp sugar
2 tsp soy sauce
1 tsp cornflour
3 tbsp oil

Method

1 Cut aubergine into slices, sprinkle with salt, put aside for 30 mins. Halve or quarter sprouts, quarter carrots, lengthwise, cut into small sections.

2 Cut peppers into strips, peel and quarter cucumber lengthwise, cut into sections, slice celery, rinse bean sprouts. Rinse aubergine slices, drain, pat dry with paper towelling and cut into strips.

3 Drop sprouts and carrots into boiling water, boil for 7 mins, rinse under cold running water, drain. Heat oil in large saucepan, fry garlic for a few seconds. Add aubergine, sprouts, carrots, peppers, and cucumber, cook, stirring for 3 mins, add celery and bean sprouts and cook another 1 min.

4 Pour off oil, add stock, cover and cook until vegetables are tender but still crisp. Mix together sugar, soy sauce and cornflour, add to pan and stir for another 2 mins.

Serves 6

Sauced Cauliflower

Ingredients

1 small cauliflower
200 ml sour cream or low-fat yoghurt
1 pkt French onion soup mix
pinch nutmeg

Method

1 Cook cauliflower whole until nearly tender, drain and cut into florets.

2 Mix together sour cream, onion soup mix and nutmeg.

3 Put cauliflower into a shallow ovenproof dish, cover with sour cream mixture, cook in moderate oven for 15–20 mins.

Serves 4.

Buttered Cucumbers

Ingredients

1 large cucumber
lemon juice
1 tbsp butter
1 tbsp snipped chives
black pepper

Method

1 Peel cucumbers thinly, cut into quarters lengthwise, cut the quarters into sections.

2 Cook in boiling water for 3 mins, drain thoroughly.

3 Return to the saucepan, add a good squeeze of lemon juice and the butter. Cover saucepan and cook gently for another 5 mins. Stir in the chives and pepper.

Serves 3.

Courgettes and Macaroni

Ingredients

100 g quick macaroni
2 tbsp oil
100 g sliced courgettes
1 medium onion, chopped very finely
2 medium tomatoes, chopped
1 clove garlic, crushed
½ tsp chopped mint
pinch dried dill
75 ml natural yogurt
75 g grated cheddar cheese

Method

1 Cook macaroni in plenty of boiling water until tender.

2 Gently fry the courgettes and onion in oil for about 5 minutes, add tomatoes, garlic, mint and dill.

3 Put lid on pan and simmer for 7 minutes, stir in yoghurt then add the cooked, drained macaroni.

4 Cook gently until the macaroni is reheated.

5 Turn into a serving dish, top with grated cheese.

Serves 3

Carrots with Raisins

Ingredients

2 medium-sized carrots
1 tbsp margarine
1 tbsp flour
1 tbsp instant powdered skimmed milk
100 ml water
50 g raisins
1 clove garlic, crushed

Method

1 Slice the prepared carrots and cook in boiling water until tender then drain. Meanwhile, melt margarine in a saucepan, stir in flour and milk, cook for 1 minute.

2 Gradually add the water and bring to boiling point, stirring constantly. Simmer for a minute, stir in raisins and garlic, then add drained carrots.

Spanish-style Beans

Ingredients

250 g green beans
1 tbsp olive oil
1 clove garlic, crushed
½ red pepper, cut into short strips
½ tbsp chopped parsley
salt, pepper

Method

1 Cut the prepared beans into sections and cook in boiling water until tender, drain. Heat olive oil, add garlic, pepper, parsley, cook gently for 1 min.

2 Add the drained beans, salt and pepper to taste, shake pan over low heat for another 1–2 mins and serve.

Serves 4.

Vegetable Stew

Ingredients

1 slice bread, crusts removed
1 medium-sized onion, chopped
3 medium-sized tomatoes, peeled and sliced
200 ml vegetable stock
1 medium-sized red pepper, cut into small cubes
220 g can butter beans
2 tsp chopped parsley

Method

1 Cut bread into dice and gently fry in oil until golden, remove from oil and drain. Add onion and tomatoes to pan and cook, stirring occasionally, until onion is tender.

2 Add stock and carrots, cover and cook gently until carrots are tender. Add pepper, drained butter beans, mint and parsley. Simmer until reheated. Turn into a serving bowl and top with the fried bread cubes.

Serves 4.

Broccoli Lyonnaise

Ingredients

250 g broccoli
1 medium-sized onion
20 g margarine
pepper

Method

1 Cut any coarse leaves from washed broccoli, trim off ends of stalks and cut a deep cross in base of any extra thick stalks.

2 Cut stalks and florets into sections, cook in a little boiling, salted water for 15 mins or until just tender, but still crisp.

3 Meanwhile, slice the onions and cook in margarine until soft but not browned.

4 Drain broccoli thoroughly, add to onions and continue cooking gently, shaking pan frequently, for 3–4 minutes. Mix in pepper. Serve.

Serves 3.

Fresh Fruit Facts

Item and availability	What to look for	Nutrition and energy	Storage	Method of cooking
Apples All year, cheapest in autumn.	Fruit should be the true variety colour, with skin free of bruises. Large apples do not keep as well as smaller	Fair source of vitamin C and dietary fibre. Eating apples 196 kJ/ 100 g, stewed apples with sugar 282 kJ/ 100 g.	Keep in vented plastic bag in cool place.	Superb raw, puréed, in a tart or strudel, preserved as apple jelly. Use for fritters or bake.
Apricots June–September.	Firm, plump, fully developed fruit with a bright apricot colour. Avoid soft or shrivelled fruit.	Fair source of vitamin C, vitamin A and dietary fibre. Some iron. 108 kJ/ 100 g raw.	Keep in unsealed plastic bag in cool place for 2–3 days. Will deteriorate quickly at room temperature.	As a snack. Use in fruit salad and jam. Cooking draws out the flavour. Serve with ham, lamb and duck.
Avocados All year.	Generally glossy and hard when unripe. When ripe skin colour is dull, and a toothpick easily pierces flesh at stem. Hass variety has rough dark skin.	Fair source of vitamin C, riboflavin and dietary fibre. Some iron, thiamin and nicotinic acid. Fair source of polyunsaturated fat. 922 kJ/100 g.	Ripen at room temperature, then store in cool place.	Use mashed on bread and sprinkle with lemon juice. Fill with seafood and dressing. Ideal accompaniment to smoked fish and as a soup. A great ice cream.
Bananas All year.	Best eating quality will be bright, medium sized fruit, yellow to gold in colour, well-rounded and free of bruises.	Fair source of vitamin A, vitamin C and dietary fibre. Some iron and thiamin. 337 kJ/100 g.	Store at room temperature to continue ripening process. Skin will blacken if refrigerated.	Sliced with cinnamon and yoghurt. Ingredient in cakes, biscuits, desserts. Blend with milk for a nourishing drink. Use for fritters.
Cherries June–August.	Firm, fresh, bright uniform-coloured fruit, with green stems.	Fair source of vitamin C and dietary fibre. Some vitamin A. 201 kJ/100 g.	Keep unsealed plastic bag in refrigerator to stop from drying out. Highly perishable. Eat soon after purchase.	Use fresh, or as a tart filling. Blend stoned cherries for fruit sauce. Combine with walnuts and chicken in salad. As a soup.

4.2 kJ = 1 kcal

Fresh Fruit Facts

Item and availability	What to look for	Nutrition and energy	Storage	Method of cooking
Grapes All year. Cheapest July–September	Select bunches of uniform shaped berries, smooth and plump with natural bloom not rubbed off. Stems should be green with fruit firmly attached.	Some vitamin C, iron and thiamin. 268 kJ/ 100 g.	In vented plastic bag in refrigerator. Use as quickly as possible.	Great as a snack. Serve with cheese or pâté, and in fruit salad, combines well with fish.
Lemons All year.	Firm and heavy fruit. Skin should be clean with fine texture.	Good source of vitamin C. Some calcium and iron. 65 kJ/100 g.	Keep in cool place. Lemon slices and juice can be frozen for use at later date.	Use as a meat tenderiser (mix with mustard to coat meat before baking) and in sorbets. Helps stop apples and bananas from discolouring.
Honeydew Melon All year. Cheapest Aug–November.	Avoid soft spots and look for a clean stem scar.	Excellent source of vitamin C. Good source of vitamin A. Fair source dietary fibre. Some iron. 90 kJ/100 g.	Ripen at room temperature for finer flavour. Wrap cut melon in plastic and store in refrigerator away from butter and milk.	Use in fruit salad, eat alone or with ice cream. Ideal as an entree, slice and serve with ham.
Oranges All year.	Firm and heavy fruit. Skin should be glossy with a fine texture. Colour does not indicate maturity.	Excellent source vitamin C. Fair source dietary fibre. Some vitamin A, thiamin and calcium. 150 kJ/100 g.	Can be kept outside refrigerator in cool place for short time. Store in a cool place.	Serve with meat, rice. Use to flavour puddings, breads, biscuits, desserts and in fruit salad, marmalade. Ideal as juice.
Passionfruit All year.	Full heavy fruit with smooth dark purple skin. Avoid withered fruit.	Excellent source of vitamin C. Fair source of vitamin A. 147 kJ/100 g.	Keep in plastic bag in crisper of refrigerator. Pulp may be frozen for later use.	Use in fruit salad and fruit punch. Serve as topping over ice cream, pavlovas and flummery or as a fruit sauce. Include in icings.

4.2 kJ = 1 kcal

Fresh Fruit Facts

Item and availability	What to look for	Nutrition and energy	Storage	Method of cooking
Peaches June–October	Firm fruit which is just beginning to soften, with a peachy smell. Avoid bruised or under-developed fruit.	Fair source of vitamin C and dietary fibre. Some vitamin A, iron, nicotinic acid. 156 kJ/100 g.	Keep in unsealed plastic bag in refrigerator. Will deteriorate quickly at room temperature.	Pies. Top with cinnamon and butter and lightly grill. Eat fresh with cereal, ice cream, cream or yoghurt. Use in compôtes and mousse.
Pears All year.	Pears ripen from the inside out after harvesting. Test for ripeness by applying gentle pressure at the stem area. Avoid immature fruit.	Fair source of vitamin C and dietary fibre. 175 kJ/100 g.	Keep in vented plastic bag in cool place. Ripen at room temperature.	Eat raw with cheese and walnuts. Preserve. Serve with roast lamb, smoked fish or ham. Poach in vanilla syrup and coat with chocolate.
Pineapples All year. Cheapest September–November.	Skin colour not a reliable guide, but in winter select fruit with quarter yellow colour and no soft spots. Look for fresh deep green leaves and pleasant aroma.	Good source of vitamin C. Fair source of dietary fibre. Some vitamin A, thiamin. 194 kJ/100 g.	Keep in cool place or in refrigerator. Refrigerate before serving if desired.	Fruit salads, upside-down cakes, with ham in salads or sandwiches. Serve with bacon as hors d'oeuvres, or with cheese or sausages. Use in Chinese cooking.
Strawberries All year. Cheapest July–September.	Fruit should be clean and brightly coloured with no sign of soft spots or mould. Look for green stem cap and avoid fruit with white or green areas.	Excellent source vitamin C. Fair source dietary fibre. Some iron. 109 kJ/100 g. ·	Keep in refrigerator. Very perishable. Use as soon possible.	Preserves, jams, tarts. Purée for fruit sauce. Combine with pineapple. Add to fruit salad. With cream or yoghurt. In fruit punch.
Watermelon August–November	Large, well-coloured bright fruit that is heavy in the hand.	Fair source of vitamin C. Some vitamin A. 92 kJ/100 g.	Store in cool place or in refrigerator. When cut, use promptly.	Great for picnics and in fruit salad, jams and pickles. Lovely as a refreshing drink.

The Apple

Nutritive Value of an Apple

In 100 g of baking apple we have:

85.6 g water
0.3 g protein
9.6 g carbohydrate (sugar)
153 mg minerals
16 mg vitamins
and 159 kJ in the edible part
(i.e. not the core or the skin).

In the vegetable section we looked at the versatility of the potato. Here we will look at its fruit counterpart, the apple.
- Prepare a selection of the following recipes and discuss your results.

Raw Apple

You can use any variety, but Granny Smith and Jonathans are the most reliable varieties of apples to use in the recipes below.
— Grate raw apple into coleslaw. Add dressing immediately.
— Dice red-skinned apple into fruit salad, cover with juices of other fruits immediately.
— Grate raw apple into just cooked, hot rhubarb.
— Eat raw apple on its own.
— Slice raw apple and mix with walnuts and mayonnaise as well as diced celery to make Waldorf salad.
— Serve a 'medley' of sliced, fresh fruits as a dessert – blanch the apple quickly.
- How many more raw apple ideas can you think of? List these in your book.

More Apple Recipes to Try

Potato-Apple Cake

Ingredients

4 large potatoes
1 large baking apple
1 small onion, grated
salt and pepper
½ tsp dried marjoram or chopped dried rosemary
2 cloves garlic, crushed
oil

Method

1 Peel potatoes and wipe with paper towel. Cut into match-thin strips about 4–5 cm long. Peel and core the apple and cut into match-thin strips the same size.
2 Put grated onion into a bowl, add potatoes, apple, salt, and pepper, marjoram and garlic. Mix well. Heat about 2 tbsp oil in a frying pan. Add potato mixture using a fork to form a cake, press down lightly.
3 Fry, lifting the edges occasionally with a fork or spatula, until browned underneath. Remove from heat and carefully turn the cake over with a fish slice. Return to heat and continue cooking until browned, adding more oil if necessary.

Serves 4.

Baked Apple

1 Wash apple, remove core, score skin. Fill core cavity with dried fruit.
2 Place in casserole with 2 tbsp water. Stab skin with 2 cloves per apple.
3 Bake at 180°C, gas mark 4 for 40–50 mins.

Serves 1.

Apple Pie

1 Line a metal pie dish with pastry (see page 61).
2 Peel and core 800 g cooking apples. Slice on to the pastry, sprinkle with 40 g sugar.
3 Cover with pastry, moistening the edges to stick. Make a hole for steam to escape. Brush with water, sprinkle with cinnamon and sugar.
4 Bake at 200'°C, gas mark 6, for 30 mins.

Serves 4

Waldorf Open Sandwich

Ingredients

1 unpeeled red apple, chopped
2 tsp lemon juice
4 spring onions, chopped
50 g walnut pieces
2 hard-boiled eggs, cut into quarters
80 ml mayonnaise
4 slices wholemeal bread with margarine
4 large lettuce leaves

Method

1 Toss apple in lemon juice then combine with onions, walnuts and eggs. Fold mayonnaise through and chill for one hour or until serving time.

2 Arrange lettuce leaves on bread and top with salad. Garnish with parsley or stuffed olives.

Pork Sausages with Apple

Ingredients

8 thin pork sausages
2 crisp red apples
200 ml canned or bottled sweet and sour sauce
(or make your own using the Sweet and Sour Pork recipe p. 158).

Method

1 Place sausages in a saucepan of water and slowly bring almost to the boil. Remove pan from heat and cover, allowing sausages to cool in the water. Cut into pieces.

2 Thread sausage and wedges of apple onto a skewer. Grill on a low heat turning until brown—about 5 mins each side.

3 Heat some sweet and sour sauce in a pan ready to serve with sausages.

Serves 4.

Potato-Apple Salad

Ingredients

3 medium-sized potatoes, boiled
1 large, crisp apple
2 tbsp lemon juice
4 large spring onions, chopped
2 sticks celery, chopped
50 ml plain yoghurt
50 ml mayonnaise
1 tbsp dried dill weed
unpeeled apple slices to garnish

Method

1 Cut freshly cooked potatoes into small dice. Peel and core apple and dice. Combine in a bowl with lemon juice, onions and celery.

2 Mix sour cream, mayonnaise and dill together, and fold into potato mixture. Chill until serving time, and garnish with slices of apple.

Serves 6.

Apple-Raisin Pie

Ingredients

2 large cooking apples, peeled, cored and thinly sliced
2 tbsp lemon juice
50 g walnuts
50 g raisins
1 tbsp light muscovado sugar
1 tbsp plain flour
½ tsp cinnamon
pinch ground ginger
½ tsp nutmeg
250 g packet shortcrust pastry
milk for glazing

Method

1 Combine apples, lemon juice, walnuts and raisins in a large bowl.

2 Mix together sugar, flour, cinnamon and nutmeg and add to apples. Toss gently to coat apples evenly.

3 Roll out just over half the pastry on a lightly-floured surface to fit a greased pie plate, 20 cm diameter. Fill with apple mixture.

4 Roll out remaining pastry to cover the top of the pie. Press edges firmly together and crimp for a decorative effect. Cut two slits in top to allow steam to escape. Brush the top with milk.

5 Bake at 180°C, gas mark 4, for 30 minutes, until pastry is golden and apples tender.

6 Serve hot with custard or cold with whipped cream or ice cream.

Serves 6

Workshop

Fruit and Vegetable Puzzle

There are twenty-six fruits and vegetables hidden in the puzzle below. When you have found them all select any four and discover where they are grown, the seasons during which they are plentiful and how they can be served as food. Make up a recipe which includes all the four you have chosen.

```
T Q C A B B A G E R X Q N V N J O K H M
D Q Y I P C H C A E P A S S E R C R Z A
I U U C S A A T L D H Z T B E C P I P N
N R A I S N J U B E N F Z W A E E P H W
D E D R N N E T L R T H Q I A L L L G A
V B L B T C O K E I O T R R D E T Z A T
J M E F D I E L G K F C U P I R X Q M W
L U E I S Z C N E X L L C C S Y A D X G
Y C K G U E O H F M W H O O E C B U A E
R U Z R M M Q V O A Z A S W L L Y H A L
O C V S E P A R G K W F N W E I X Q T Q
C R V L H Q C A W Z E Z Z H E R L Z E S
I G H D B U K O V L I A K P B D Z C P B
H F I S U G A R A P S A G U E R E O Z C
C F U G L F A U B E R G I N E A T S S G
D Z O A I A L F X J G P R A C A Y O H X
I T D C Q F S P L U M I O I T Y H C U R
L T X Y R R E H C D F E K O X B Q K P J
```

Meat

Nutritive value

Meats are rich sources of protein and they supply good, but varying, amounts of iron, thiamin, riboflavin and nicotinic acid. Meat can also, however, supply high amounts of fat—mostly saturated fat. Cuts vary enormously in nutritional value but some typical values are:

Meat	per 100 g				
	kJ (kcal)	water g	protein g	fat g	iron mg
Lamb					
average, raw	1377 (333)	54.4	14.6	30.5	1.4
leg, roast (lean only)	800 (191)	61.8	29.4	8.1	2.7
Beef					
average, raw	1168 (282)	58.6	15.8	24.3	1.9
mince, stewed	955 (229)	59.5	23.1	15.2	3.1
Pork					
average, raw	1397 (338)	50.7	13.6	31.5	0.9
chops, grilled, (lean and fat)	1380 (332)	46.3	28.5	24.2	1.2
Chicken					
raw, meat	508 (121)	74.4	20.5	4.3	0.7
roast, meat only	621 (141)	68.4	24.8	5.4	0.8

Lamb

Cut	Cooking method
Leg	Roast, slice and grill
Loin	Grill, crumb and fry
Chop (best end of neck)	Grill
Breast	Bone, stuff and roll, then roast
Shoulder	Roast, slice and grill or braise

Lamb cuts

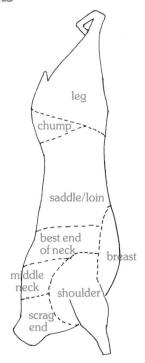

Beef cuts

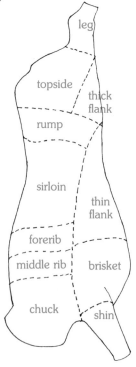

Beef

Cut	Cooking method
Shin, Clod and leg	Stew, casserole, soup
Topside Sirloin Rib	Roast or slice (steaks) and grill
Brisket	Braise or boil
Chuck	Braise or stew

Pork

Cut	Cooking method
Leg	Roast
Fillet	Roast or slice (steaks) and grill
Loin	Roast or slice (chops) and grill
Belly	Grill
Spare rib Blade	Roast, braise or stew
Shoulder	Roast, casserole, stew

Pork Cuts

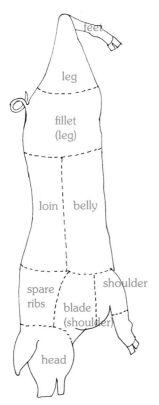

Offal is the name given to liver, kidney, heart, tongue etc. from cattle, lamb and pigs. All are nutritious, with considerably less fat than other cuts. They are also economical and tasty. Offal must be cooked or frozen soon after purchase because it goes off quickly.

Fish is a rich protein source. The term covers white fish, which has virtually no fat, fatty fish and shellfish. All types are extremely perishable, even in a refrigerator, so must be cooked soon after buying. Frozen fish should not be thawed before cooking.

Fish	Cooking method	Composition			
		energy kJ (kcal)	water g	protein g	fat g
White fish					
Cod	fried in batter	834 (199)	60.9	19.6	10.3
Haddock	steamed (or microwaved)	417 (98)	75.1	22.8	0.8
Plaice	fried in crumbs	951 (228)	59.9	18.0	13.7
Fatty fish					
Kipper	baked	855 (205)	58.7	25.5	11.4
Salmon	steamed (or microwaved)	823 (197)	65.4	20.1	13.0
Shellfish					
Prawns	boiled	451 (107)	70.0	22.6	1.8
Cockles	boiled	203 (48)	78.9	11.3	0.3

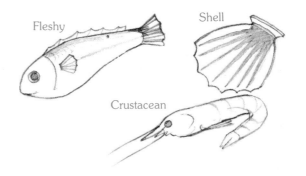

Fleshy   Shell

Crustacean

Workshop

1 Discuss as a class other meats that are eaten occasionally. Why are they not eaten often?

2 Read the recipes at the end of this workshop and answer the questions about each recipe. Prepare them if possible.

3 **What is it?**
   (This activity includes areas up to and including this chapter.)
   a It is an important substance used by the body. It helps to prevent infection. It is necessary for collagen formation.
   b It is readily available to those who eat dairy foods. It is necessary for hard bones.
   c It cooks food very quickly. It uses electrical power, is not suitable for all cooking. It thaws food well.
   d It is orange, conical in shape, a vegetable and the root of a plant.
   e It has many leaves which are varying shades of green, the darker ones being on its outer layers. It can be eaten raw or cooked. It keeps well in a cool place and is used to make coleslaw.
   f It is carried around in the bloodstream by a protein. It is important for healthy blood and for getting oxygen to body cells.
   g It is a method of cooking by dry heat in a hot enclosed space.
   h It is almost round. It has a core and pips. Its stem looks too weak to hold it. It can be red or green and sometimes yellowish. It contains about 85 per cent water and a fair amount of fibre.
   i It is the amount of energy your body needs to live. It does not take conscious activity into account. It is influenced by your age and sex and particularly your skin surface area.
   j It is a medium-sized animal, you can wear its coat and eat its flesh. Its leg is delicious roasted and served with mint sauce.

Recipes to Try

Beef Stroganoff

Ingredients

100 g rump steak
20 g margarine
½ small onion, finely chopped
75 g small mushroom, sliced
1 tbsp water
⅓ beef stock cube
1 tsp tomato paste
75 ml sour cream or low-fat plain yoghurt (this will reduce kJ content)
½ tsp cornflour

Method

1 Remove any fat from meat and cut it into thin strips about 5 mm thick, 2 cm wide and 5 cm long.

2 Heat half the margarine in a frying pan, add meat and cook on high heat until golden brown. Remove meat from pan.

3 Add remaining margarine to pan, add onion and cook until golden, add mushrooms and cook for 2 mins.

4 Return meat to pan, add crumbled cube and tomato paste and mix evenly. Simmer for 5 mins.

5 Blend cornflour and cream or yoghurt. Gradually add to meat, stirring until the mixture boils and thickens.

6 Reduce heat and simmer uncovered for 5 mins.

7 Serve with tagliatelli.

Serves 1.

Tagliatelle

Ingredients

50 g tagliatelle pasta (ribbons)
½ tsp oil
large saucepan of boiling water
½ tsp chopped parsley
1 tbsp melted margarine

Method

1 Add oil to boiling water, when it returns to the boil add the pasta and boil as rapidly as possible for 15 mins. Stir occasionally to keep pieces separate.

2 When cooked, drain through a colander.

3 Mix parsley and margarine through pasta and serve.

Serves 1.

Questions about the recipe

1 In what way does the tagliatelle 'balance' the meal?

2 Would this recipe be suitable for an individual wishing to reduce the fat content of their diet?

3 Discover the country of origin of stroganoff.

4 If you wanted to reduce the cost of the recipe by using topside steak in place of rump steak, how much would you save per serving? How would this change influence the cooking time?

Chicken Escalope

Ingredients

2 chicken escalopes (fillets)
50 g flour
3 shakes black pepper
pinch oregano
1 egg, beaten
1 tbsp water
3 tbsp sunflower oil
pinch oregano
125 ml oil

Garnish

1 hard-boiled egg
1 tbsp chopped parsley
4 rolled anchovies

Method

1 Beat the meat on an oiled board or between two sheets of oiled plastic wrap until it is of even thinness.

2 Mix flour, pepper and oregano. Coat meat with this mixture.

3 Beat egg and water together, coat meat with egg mixture then coat with breadcrumbs.

4 Heat oil gently. Fry each escalope until golden brown on each side (5–10 mins each piece depending on thickness). Cooking the meat too fast will cause it to shrink and burn on the outside leaving the inside raw. Drain on absorbent pepper.

5 Serve on a warm plate and garnish each escalope with a slice of hard-boiled egg, chopped parsley and an anchovy.

Serves 2.

Questions about the recipe

1 What could you serve with the escalope to make up a healthy meal?

2 What function(s) does the breadcrumb coating perform in this dish?

3 Modify the recipe in some way so that it can still be called escalope but so that it has your personal touch — call it Escalope... (your name).

Cereals

Nutritive Value

Cereals are all rich in carbohydrate. Those which are from the whole grain contain a lot of fibre, which is important for the smooth passage of food through the body. They are generally very good sources of thiamin. Whole cereals are also reasonably good sources of riboflavin and niacin as well as iron. Cereals contains about 12% protein.

Wheat

Type of Product	Processing	Cooking	kJ per 100 g* (kcal)
White flour	Finely milled endosperm of grain	Biscuits, breads, dumplings, cakes, pastries, thickening sauces, etc.	1493 (350)
Wholemeal flour	The whole grain finely ground	Biscuits, pastries, cakes, loaves, and bread	1351 (318)
Bourghul (can be spelt Burghul, also called Bulgur)	The whole grain is partly cooked until grains are about to burst, then dried and coarsely ground	Used in many Middle Eastern dishes such as Tabbouleh (see recipe page 135) Kibla, Felafel, as well as bread etc.	1400 (329)
Semolina	Endosperm ground to a 'gritty' texture	Puddings, cakes and biscuits biscuits	1489 (350)
Cous Cous	Tiny pellets processed from semolina and water	As accompaniment to meat and vegetable dishes	1300 (306)
Pastas	A variety of different shapes made from a wheat flour paste and dried	All noodle, spaghetti, canneloni, lasagne, ravioli, tagliatelli, etc. dishes (pasta is boiled)	1612 (378)
Buckwheat	A member of the dock and rhubarb family, the same in carbohydrate and kilojoules as wheat, but slightly different in other nutrients.	Pancakes, biscuits, breads	1200 (282)
Buckwheat flour	As above, milled to a fine flour	Blinis (see recipe page 135), breads loaves	1440 (339)

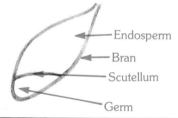

Endosperm
Bran
Scutellum
Germ

Corn

Type of Product	Processing	Cooking	kJ per 100 g* (kcal)
Corn on the cob	The whole 'fruit' of the corn plant	Leaves removed, boiled	520
Canned kernels (whole or creamed)	Seeds removed from cob, cooked and preserved in cans	Soups, salads, as a vegetable, pancakes	(123) 325
Popping corn	Dried corn kernels (seeds)	Heated in a little oil until grain bursts open	(76)

*all values uncooked except corn

Type of Product	Processing	Cooking	kJ per 100 g* (kcal)
Polenta	Coarsely ground corn kernels	Dumplings, vegetable casseroles	1474 (347)
Cornflour	Finely milled from the endosperm of the grain (though this is often made from the starch of the endosperm of wheat)	Thickens sauces, used in cakes and biscuits	1508 (354)

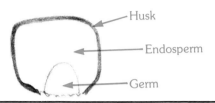

Rice

Type of Product	Processing	Cooking	kJ per 100 g* (kcal)
Long grain, brown	The whole grain	As an accompaniment to a meat dish especially those with very highly flavoured sauces such as sweet and sour or curry; also used in desserts, casseroles, soups; is boiled in water — can be fried first	1536 (361) approx.
Short grain, brown	The whole grain		
Long grain, polished	The bran removed		
Short grain, polished	The bran removed		
Rice flour	Polished rice milled to a 'gritty' texture	A gluten-free flour used in biscuits, particularly shortbread	1478 (352)

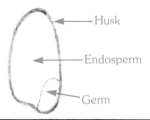

Oats

Type of Product	Processing	Cooking	kJ per 100 g* (kcal)
Rolled Oats	Coarsely rolled whole grain	Porridge, cakes, loaves, biscuits	1698 (401)
Oatmeal	Milled a little more than rolled oats	Breads, scones, porridge, pancakes, loaves	
Quick Oats	Treated oatmeal for quick cooking	Porridge, biscuits	

*uncooked

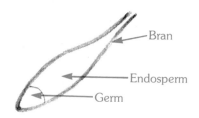

Oat grain

Bran
Endosperm
Germ

Barley

Type of Product	Processing	Cooking	kJ per 100 g* (kcal)
Pearl barley	The whole grain with a little husk removed	Soups, barley water	1535 (360)
Barley meal	Milled whole grain	Add to bread for flavour	1482 (354)

Bran
Endosperm
Germ

Rye

Type of Product	Processing	Cooking	kJ per 100g (kcal)
Rye flour	The whole grain	Bread, loaves	1428 (335)

Endosperm
Bran
Germ

When considering cereals for your diet remember wholegrain cereals are the best ones to eat. Cereal foods should make up quite a large portion of your daily diet (they are one of the 'Eat Most' foods).

If you are not keen on wholegrain cereals you must eat fruits and vegetables (raw and cooked) for fibre and carbohydrate, a little iron and B group vitamins. You would need extra meat or nuts for the B vitamins and iron as well as protein.

Wholegrain cereals are the best dietary source of thiamin and wheat provides the most useful fibre for the body.

*uncooked

Workshop

1 Make up a selection of the recipes from those following Investigation
   no. 18. Answer the questions about the recipes and write up
   the details of the properties of each of the cereals you used in the
   recipes.

2 **Puzzle**
   Discover the word which fits in these squares:

Each of the following words have at least two letters in common with it
and help to define it.
   Grass, Fibre, Energy, Edible, Corn

Investigation No. 18
The Properties of Cereals

Aim
● To discover the appearance, texture and the reaction to moisture and
  heat of a number of milled cereals

Procedure
a Collect as many flours as you can, for example plain wheat flour, S.R.
   wheat flour, wholemeal flour, S.R. wholemeal flour, rice flour, polenta,
   semolina, arrowroot, cornflour, buckwheat flour, rye flour.
b Examine each for texture—collect a pinch between your fingers and
   describe the feel. Record the result for each. Record your observation
   of its appearance—for example, fine, white, powdery, coarse,
   flecked.
c Measure one level tablespoon of each flour into a small container, add
   one level tablespoon of water and mix together evenly. Observe the
   differences in the mixtures, for example, thick and rough, smooth and
   creamy, watery.

d Light an oven on 190°C, gas mark 5. Grease enough of a bun tray so you have one section for each sample. Draw a quick sketch of the tray. Put one sample into each section and record on your sketch which sample is in which section. For example:

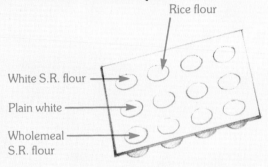

Rice flour

White S.R. flour

Plain white

Wholemeal
S.R. flour

e Bake your samples for 10 minutes.

f Remove tray and record results from immediate observation — for example, risen to a peak, rough, dry and unrisen, clear and glassy.

g Remove each sample from the tray and press gently for texture. Record results — for example, springy, hard, rubbery, gelatinous.

h Cut each sample in half and examine the texture — for example, doughy, paste-like, aerated like a scone, dry and hard.
Your results should be tabulated in some way. You can use the table below for guidance.

Sample	Observation	Feel	Water absorbancy	Cooked appearance	Cooked texture	Cut texture
White flour						

Discussion/Conclusion

— Which flours readily absorb water?
— Which flours are the most useful for cake making?
— Which flours are suitable for biscuits and pastries?
— Which flours are not suitable for baking?
— Which flours are better suited to thickening or setting a liquid?
— Was there any characteristic of the wheat flours that separated them from the rest, for example, in cooked texture?
— Which recipes would usually require a greater proportion of liquid to flour?

Recipes to Try

Tabouli (Tabbouleh)

Ingredients

50 g bourghul soaked in cold water for 45 mins
50 g chopped parsley
tbsp chopped mint
tbsp chopped spring onions

Dressing

2 tbsp lemon juice
4–6 tbsp olive oil
salt and freshly ground pepper
2 chopped tomatoes

Method

1 Mix together the drained bourghul, parsley, mint and spring onions.

2 Make a dressing by whisking together the lemon juice and the oil and seasoning it with salt and pepper.

3 Pour dressing over salad mixture and cover with a plate or put a lid on the bowl. Holding plate firmly over bowl, shake the salad thoroughly up and down and round and round, so that the dressing is thoroughly mixed into the salad.

4 Pile the tabouli into a serving bowl and garnish with the chopped tomatoes. Chill for 15 mins.

Serves 3.

Questions about the recipe

1 What is the cereal in this recipe? Where does it come from?

2 Find two other recipes that use this same cereal.

3 Which nutrients need to be supplied by those foods served with the tabouli to make a healthy meal?

4 This particular salad is very popular at the moment. See if you can come up with two reasons why this is so.

Blinis

Ingredients

50 g buckwheat flour
50 g white flour
1/4 tsp salt
10 g fresh yeast
150 ml luke-warm skimmed milk
1 egg, separated
1 tbsp melted margarine
1 tbsp oil

Accompaniments

2 hard-boiled eggs (Place eggs in cold water, bring to boil, simmer 10 mins. Pour off hot water, run cold water over and crack the shells to prevent a grey layer around yolk.)
4 spring onions
150 ml sour cream or plain yoghurt

These are the traditional accompaniments; the egg and onion could be replaced with fresh or cooked fruit.

Method

1 Chop eggs and onions finely and chill in separate covered bowls.

2 Mix flours and salt.

3 Mix yeast to a cream with a little of the warm milk, then add remaining milk.

4 Stir the yeast liquid into the flours to make a smooth batter. Leave covered in a warm place until it has doubled in size – about 20–30 mins.

5 Mix the batter again, knocking it back to its original size. Add the egg yolk and margarine and mix evenly.

6 Whip the egg white and fold into the mixture.

7 Heat griddle or frying pan to a moderately slow heat. Brush pan with oil.

8 Spoon batter onto the hot surface about 2 tbsp at a time to make blinis 10 cm in diameter. When the mixture sets and the surface is covered with broken bubbles, turn it over and cook the other side. Keep blinis warm.

9 Serve with chopped hard-boiled eggs, onion and cream or yoghurt each in separate bowls. Each diner helps himself to a hot blini, covers it with egg, onion and yoghurt, then placed another blini on top. Eat with a knife and.fork.

Serves 2.

Questions about the recipe

1 What is the function of the yeast in the recipe? How does it perform this function?

2 In what other form(s) can buckwheat be purchased?

3 Suggest other accompaniments you could serve with blinis.

4 Find out the country of origin of this recipe.

Dinner Dumplings

Ingredients

150 g S.R. flour
¼ tsp baking powder
2 tsp wheat germ
50 g grated cheese
2 shakes onion salt
1 slice ham, chopped
2 tsp chopped parsley
1 pinch mixed herbs
1 egg
60 ml milk

Sauce

1 chicken cube
200 ml boiling water
2 tsp tomato paste

Method

1 Sift flour and baking powder together.

2 Mix together all ingredients to a soft dough (not sauce ingredients).

3 Knead lightly.

4 Divide the mixture into 8 equal portions and roll each into a ball. Place in a greased casserole dish allowing plenty of room for the dumplings to rise.

5 Mix all the sauce ingredients together and pour around the dumplings.

6 Cover casserole and bake in a hot oven at 220°C, gas mark 7 for 15–20 mins or until dumplings have doubled their size and are light and spongy to the touch.

Serves 4.

Questions about the recipe

1 If you served these dumplings with baked lamb chops, which other vegetables (if any) would you need to serve to make a healthy meal?

2 Which nutrients are provided by the dumplings?

3 At what time of the year would dumplings be the most welcome for dinner?

4 Can you suggest why German people frequently serve dumplings?

Stuffed Parathas

Ingredients

100 g wholemeal flour
½ tbsp margarine, melted
3 tbsp water (approx.)
oil for frying

Filling ingredients

2 or 3 small cauliflower florets, finely chopped
½ tsp cumin seeds   } mixed together
½ tsp ground coriander
pinch chilli powder

Method

1 Mix flour, margarine and water. Knead until a soft dough is formed.

2 Make two even-sized balls.

3 Make a depression in each of the balls and put 1 tsp of the filling in each. Pull dough over the filling a roll again into a ball.

4 Roll each paratha on a lightly-floured board to a 15 c round.

5 Heat oil in frying pan. Fry a paratha over low heat un brown on the bottom (about 5 mins). Turn carefully and fry the other side for a further 3 mins until golden.

Serves 2

Questions about the recipe

1 From which country did this recipe originally come?

2 What other fillings can you suggest?

3 The paratha is cooked in a similar way to pancakes—what is the difference between a paratha and the pancakes traditionally eaten on Shrove Tuesday?

4 What main dish might parathas accompany?

Quiche Rolls

Base Ingredients

50 g SR wholemeal flour
tbsp margarine
80 ml milk

Method

Preheat oven to 220°C, gas mark 7.

Rub margarine into flour until mixture resembles fine breadcrumbs.

Add water, turn onto floured board and knead until smooth.

Roll out to a rectangular shape, about 25 cm × 20 cm.

Spread filling on centre, leaving 2 cm at each side.

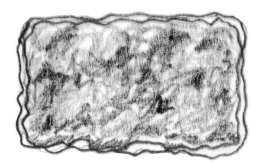

Roll up.

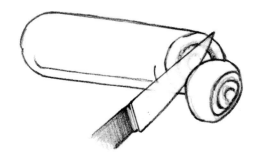

Cut into 3 cm slices.

8 Place on a lightly greased tray and cook until brown on top and bottom (approximately 15 mins).

Filling Ingredients

1 egg
50 g grated cheese
1 onion, finely chopped
1 rasher bacon or slice of ham
pepper

Method

1 Finely chop ham or bacon and fry until crisp, add onion and fry until clear. Take off heat and cool.

2 Beat egg and add to cheese and mix well.

3 Add onions, bacon and pepper to taste.

More About Cereals

There are two very important cereal products that are a part of the diet of many of the world's people. These two products, **bread** and **pasta,** deserve a slightly closer look than has been given them in the previous section.

Bread

Bread is often called the 'staff of life', a staff being something to guide with or something to support. Bread in all shapes and forms, provides a very important supporting role in the meals of many people.

The main ingredient in bread is cereal flour of one type or another. Frequently the bread includes a mixture of flours and cracked grains. Sometimes other ingredients are added such as dried fruits, milk, eggs, cheese, vegetables and seeds such as sesame or poppy.

Most breads we think of straight away include yeast as an ingredient. Yeast is a raising agent (leavening agent) used in all sorts of bread. There are, however, very many unleavened breads and loaves of various flavours that are called bread.

There are three types of yeast used in the recipes at the end of this section. Fresh yeast or compressed yeast is creamy in colour, feels cool and moist to the touch and has a pleasant smell, it should be blended with warm liquid before being added to the dough. Dried yeast is more concentrated than fresh yeast and so a smaller amount is needed, use half the weight of fresh yeast stated in a recipe. Dried yeast should be mixed with warm liquid and a teaspoon of sugar and should be allowed to stand for 10 minutes until it is frothy. This shows that the yeast is working. If the mixture does not froth it should not be used. Easyblend dried yeast is very simple to use: it is added to the flour before any other ingredients are added. For all types of dried yeast, always follow the instructions on the packet.

Nutritive value

Bread is a high carbohydrate food that supplies the body with energy, B vitamins and protein. When selecting bread, choose high fibre, wholegrain or wholemeal bread to obtain the fibre your body needs. Wheat provides the most useful fibre for the body — the fibre capable of high water absorbency.

Pasta

If you tried to eat your way through all the different kinds of pasta dishes, you could taste a new one every week for the next four years. The pasta family ranges from the familiar spaghetti, macaroni and lasagne to butterfly shapes called *farfalle*, shells called *conchiglie* and ribbons called *tagliatelle*.

Pasta is basically a mixture of coarsely ground durum wheat and water. The paste is pressed into plain or fancy shapes, which give it its name, and then it is dried.

- Is there any difference between noodles and pasta? See what you can come up with in a class discussion then research the labels of both products.

Pasta can be served countless ways by varying the sauces which accompany it. They range from the popular tomato sauce to sauces of shellfish, chicken livers, anchovies or mushrooms. Sauces should be put on each individual serving and grated Parmesan or Romano cheese sprinkled on top. It takes a little practice to eat the long pastas such as spaghetti. The correct method is to wind the pasta on to a fork while holding the end of the fork in the bowl of a spoon — this requires practice and a nimble wrist!

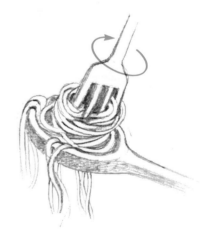

When cooking pasta, it should be boiled in lots of water so that it can move freely in the saucepan to discourage the pieces from sticking together. It should still be fairly firm when cooked, that is, it should not break easily. Cooking time varies depending on the type of pasta being used.

Workshop

1 Research the difference in nutritive value between wholemeal bread, brown bread, white bread, enriched white bread and white high-fibre bread (the fibre used is soya bean husks).

If you did not do Investigation No. 9 in chapter 3, 'Resource Savers in the Kitchen', it is suggested that you work through it here. You could either compare the efficiency of appliances in cooking bread or you could compare white and wholemeal bread in the same oven (see recipes following this workshop), or both.

Make up a selection of the flat and loaf breads at the end of this workshop. Discuss the ways they are served and discover, where possible, the country of origin.

Draw up your own 'Pasta Glossary' by collecting as many shapes as possible, describe them with words and drawings and their correct name.

We frequently think of pasta as belonging to Italy. Find out which countries serve pasta frequently — search through books on food habits of other cultures.

There is a never-ending supply of pasta recipes. There are some following the bread recipes and some elsewhere in this book. Prepare a pasta buffet, label each dish and sample as many as possible. Which was your favourite? Why? Which recipe did you like but think it would be better if ...?

Bread Recipes

White Bread

Ingredients

00 g plain flour
tsp salt (optional)
sachet easyblend dried yeast.
00 ml warm water (approximately)
5 g margarine

Wholemeal Bread

Ingredients

00 g wholemeal flour
50 g plain flour
tsp salt (optional)
sachet easyblend dried yeast
225 ml warm water (approximately)
5 g margarine

Method (for white and wholemeal bread)

1 Mix dry ingredients including yeast in a large bowl. Rub in margarine.

2 Pour warm water into dry ingredients. Beat well with wooden spoon until most of the flour is taken up. Then mix the dough by hand until all flour is mixed in.

3 Turn on to a lightly floured board. Knead 10 mins. Lightly grease the bowl and return dough, cover and leave in a warm place to double its size — about 35 mins (45 mins for wholemeal).

4 Punch fist into centre of risen dough. Draw edges to the centre to form a ball. Knead 1 min on lightly floured board.

5 Shape into a loaf and place in greased bread tin. Brush top of loaf with a little warm water, cover and leave to rise until it doubles its size again — about 25 mins (35 mins for wholemeal).

6 Very gently brush top with warm water. Bake at 230°C, gas mark 8 for 35 mins. Cool on a wire rack when cooked.

Note: The first proving in step 3 may be omitted to save time. These recipes can also be used to make rolls.

Yeast Buns

Ingredients

30 g compressed yeast
75 g sugar
500 g plain flour
375 ml milk

1 tsp salt
1½ tsp cinnamon
50 g margarine
50 g sultanas
1 egg
50 g currants
1½ tsp mixed spice

Method

1 Crumble yeast into a medium bowl and mix with 1 tsp each of the measured sugar and flour

2 Heat milk to lukewarm and add to yeast mixture.

3 Cover and stand in a warm place for 15–20 mins until foamy.

4 Sift remaining flour, sugar, salt, mixed spice and cinnamon into a large bowl. Rub margarine into this mixture until it resembles breadcrumbs.

5 Stir in the dried fruit. Beat the egg and add it to the yeast mixture then make a well in the dry ingredients and add the liquids to mix to a soft elastic dough (should be very soft, but not too sticky to handle).

6 Turn the dough on to a floured board and knead well. Kneading is a very important part of bread making. The dough should be kneaded strongly until the gluten in the flour is developed sufficiently so that the dough springs back after you make an indentation with your finger.

7 Put the dough back into the bowl and cover with clingfilm. Stand the dough to prove in a warm place until it has doubled in size (approximately 30–45 mins).

8 Punch the dough down; knead lightly until smooth.

9 Divide into 18 pieces and knead each portion into a round shape. Place each bun on to a greased tray leaving about 3–4 cm between each so they will join together when cooking. Prove the dough again by covering the buns with clingfilm and leaving for 15–20 mins in a warm place until they have nearly doubled in bulk. If making Hot Cross Buns, pipe crosses on now (see below).

10 Bake in a hot oven 220°C, gas mark 7 for 10 mins then 200°C, gas mark 6 for 10 mins.

11 Remove from oven and glaze with the following mixture to give the characteristic shine.
The buns will freeze well.

Glaze

Combine 1 tbsp sugar, 1 tbsp water and ½ tsp mixed spice and heat until boiling. Brush over the hot, cooked buns.

Hot Cross Buns

Mix 75 g flour with 65 ml water to make a smooth paste. Using a piping bag, pipe crosses on each bun after you have arranged them all on the baking tray, that is before they are baked.

Note: The first proving may be omitted to save time.

Muffins

Ingredients

425 g plain flour *or*
200 g plain and 225 g wholemeal
½ rounded tsp salt (optional)
1 tsp margarine
1 sachet dried yeast
320 ml warm water
½ tsp sugar

Method

1 Blend water, yeast and sugar and set aside in a warm place until frothy.

2 Sift flour and salt and rub in the margarine, mix to a soft dough with yeast mixture.

3 Knead a little until smooth. Place back into the bowl cover and stand in a warm place until doubled in size — about 40 mins.

4 Knead lightly and divide into 70 g pieces (weigh on scales).

5 Shape each into a flat round on a board dusted with flour or rice flour.

6 Place on a greased tray allowing 5–6 cm between each. Cover and leave in a warm place to double in size — about 15–20 mins.

7 Bake in a hot oven 230°C, gas mark 8 for 10 mins. Remove tray and quickly turn each muffin over. Return to the oven for a further 10 mins.

8 To serve, split in half when cold, toast and butter.

Makes 10.

Pitta Bread.

Ingredients

225 g wholemeal flour
1/2 tsp salt
15 g compressed yeast or 1 sachet dried yeast
1/2 tsp raw brown sugar
150 ml warm water
1 tbsp vegetable oil

Method

1 Sift flour and salt into a bowl — return bran.

2 Crumble yeast into a small bowl and add sugar and water. Leave in a warm place about 20 mins until frothy.

3 Add yeast to flour and mix to a soft dough. Knead on a lightly floured board until it is smooth and elastic (about 10 mins).

4 Pour oil into a warm bowl and turn the dough in it until it is coated all over, cover and leave in a warm place for about 20 mins or until it has doubled in size.

5 Knock back the dough and knead on a lightly floured surface until all the oil is kneaded in. Divide into 8 equal portions for small pitta, 4 for larger pitta and roll each into a round about 7 mm thick. Place on greased trays, cover and leave in a warm place for 15 mins to rise. Bake at 200°C, gas mark 6 for 7–10 mins until well risen and just coloured.

Chapatis

Ingredients

150 g wholemeal flour
150 g plain flour
1/2 tsp salt
200 ml lukewarm water
shallow frying oil

Method

1 Mix flours, salt and water to form a stiff dough.

2 Turn on to a lightly floured board and knead until dough is elastic to the touch (approximately 10 mins)

3 Cover and set aside for 1 hour

4 Form dough into balls, roll out thinly and cut into circles with large cutter (about 15 cm).

5 Fry in hot, shallow oil until they puff up and are golden brown.

Poori (Puri)

Ingredients

500 g wholemeal flour
cold water
deep frying oil

Method

1 Mix flour with water to make a soft, pliable, but not sticky dough.

2 Knead well. Place back into bowl and cover with a damp cloth for 1 hour.

3 Knead again until the dough is smooth and does not stick to the hands.

4 Make into balls the size of egg. Roll these out on a floured board until they are the size of a saucer.

5 Heat deep fryer to 380°C. Cook one poori at a time, giving each a gentle push with a wooden spoon as it cooks — this encourages it to puff out. Turn and cook until pale golden.

6 Drain and keep hot or serve at once.

French Bread or Rolls

Ingredients

150 ml lukewarm milk
150 ml lukewarm water
1 tsp soft brown sugar
20 g compressed yeast
450 g white flour
1 tsp salt
2 tbsp melted margarine (40 g)

Method

1 Mix together the milk, water, sugar and yeast and leave in a warm place for about 15 mins, or until frothy.

2 Add this to the sifted flour and salt and stir until most of the flour is mixed in.

3 Turn out on to a floured board and knead, with floured hands, for 10 mins to a soft dough.

4 Pour 1 tbsp of melted margarine into a warm bowl and put the dough into it, turning it over to coat it all with the margarine. Cover and leave in a warm place for 40–50 mins until it has doubled in size.

5 Knead for 3 mins. Shape into a long sausage, place on a greased tray and leave in a warm place until well risen. Cut slashes on top and bake for 20 mins at 220°C. Glaze the top with the remaining butter 5 mins before it is cooked.

Alternatively:

For bread rolls, divide the dough into 18 equal sized pieces after the second kneading. Shape each piece into a roll — can be rolled and tied into a knot, plaited, twisted, etc. Allow to prove until doubled in size. Bake at 220°C, gas mark 7 for 14–20 mins and glaze as for bread.

Pasta Recipes

Wholemeal Spaghetti, Venetian Style

Ingredients

200 g wholemeal spaghetti
125 g can sardines in tomato sauce
2 tbsp oil
freshly ground black pepper

Method

1 Cook spaghetti in boiling water until tender.

2 When almost cooked, chop sardines in small pieces and heat in olive oil. Crush with a fork to make a smooth sauce.

3 Drain spaghetti and place in a heated bowl. Pour sardines over, toss to combine and sprinkle black pepper over the top. Serve with a mixed salad.

Serves 4.

Pasta Salad

Ingredients

125 g pasta shapes, shells or spirals
1 large tomato, chopped
50 g shredded cabbage
½ an apple grated
3 tbsp mayonnaise
1 or 2 spring onions chopped

Method

1 Cook pasta in plenty of boiling water for 20 mins. Drain and cool.

2 Place pasta in a bowl and toss in dressing. Add vegetables and apple and toss lightly. Chill and serve.

Serves 4.

Penne Florentine

(This Florentine sauce is delicious with either penne pasta or with elbow macaroni.)

Ingredients

250 ml milk
1 bay leaf
1 large slice onion
25 g margarine
25 g plain flour
pepper and nutmeg to taste
125 g pkt chopped spinach, thawed
50 g grated cheese
125 g penne or macaroni
extra grated cheese to serve

Method

1 Bring milk to the boil with bay leaf and onion. Cover and put aside to infuse for 10 mins.

2 Melt butter in a saucepan and stir in flour. Cook for 1 min, stirring, then remove from heat. Slowly stir in strained milk until smooth. Return to heat and stir until sauce is thickened. Season with pepper and nutmeg.

3 Stir in spinach and grated cheese and allow to simmer very gently for 3 mins.

4 Meanwhile, cook penne or macaroni in plenty of boiling salted water until tender. Drain and arrange in a heated serving bowl. Spoon sauce over and toss gently to combine. Serve with extra grated cheese sprinkled on top.

Serves 4.

Quick Lasagne

Ingredients

2 tbsp vegetable oil
2 cloves garlic, crushed
1 large onion, finely chopped
5 large ripe tomatoes, peeled and chopped
freshly ground pepper to taste
6–8 sheets lasagne*
250 g mozzarella or Cheddar cheese, cut into thin slices
2 tbsp grated parmesan cheese

Method

1 Heat the oil and sauté garlic and onion until soft. Add tomatoes and cook very gently, stirring often, until tomatoes are soft. Season with pepper.

2 Purée sauce in a blender or push through a sieve.

3 Place alternate layers of sauce, lasagne and cheese in a shallow, greased casserole dish, beginning and ending with sauce. Sprinkle top with grated cheese and bake in a moderate oven for 30 mins or until pasta is soft and cheese is golden. Serve with buttered spinach or a tossed green salad.

Serves 6.

*Lasagne used in this recipe must be the type which needs no pre-cooking.

Buttered Pasta

Ingredients

250 g spaghetti
2 tbsp oil
60 g butter or margarine
2–3 cloves garlic, crushed
2 tbsp very finely chopped parsley
1 tsp dried oregano
¼ tsp dried rosemary
150 ml cream or low-fat natural yoghurt
pepper to taste

Method

1 Cook spaghetti in plenty of boiling water, with oil added, until just tender.

2 Just before spaghetti is ready, heat butter gently in another saucepan and fry garlic until golden (don't let it brown)

3 Stir herbs and cream or yoghurt into garlic butter and heat gently.

4 Drain spaghetti well and return to saucepan. Pour cream mixture over and sprinkle with freshly ground pepper. Toss spaghetti until coated with the sauce, transfer it all to a heated bowl and serve at once.

Serves 4.

Tagliatelle à la Papalina

Ingredients

25 g margarine
200 g sliced mushrooms
6 slices ham, cut into strips
1 small onion, finely chopped
1 clove garlic, crushed
pinch of pepper
4 egg yolks
25 g grated parmesan cheese
50 g margarine, melted
1 tbsp fresh lemon juice
250 g tagliatelle noodles, cooked and drained
2 tbsp chopped parsley
3 tbsp grated parmesan cheese

Method

1 Melt 25 g margarine in a large saucepan. Add mushrooms, ham, onion and garlic and sauté for 5 mins. Add pepper to taste.

2 Combine egg yolks and parmesan cheese, stir in melted butter and lemon juice. Combine ham mixture with sauce and pour over noodles. Sprinkle with parsley and parmesan cheese and serve.

Serves 4–6.

143

Herbs and Spices

Herbs

Most herbs are aromatic leaves of small plants added to food to enhance the flavour. Herbs can be home grown and used fresh or bought in the dried form. They should be purchased in small quantities and kept air tight as they do lose their flavour. Herbs can also be used as a replacement for salt in many recipes.

Some popular herbs

Apple Mint: One of the most fragrant members of the mint family. The green leaves are used in sauces, salads and vegetable dishes.

Basil: Has a sweet, pungent, aromatic flavour and blends well with tomato. Try it with other vegetables also.

Bay: Rather large leaves used to flavour meat and vegetable dishes.

Borage: Has a distinct cucumber flavour, used in drinks.

Chervil: Tiny leaves with a fresh spicy flavour. Blends well in an omelette or other egg dishes as well as salad.

Chives: A member of the onion family but we just snip off the thin grass-like tops. Has a mild onion flavour which blends well with egg, cottage cheese or salads or to garnish vegetables such as jacket potatoes.

Dillweed: The feathery leaves of dillweed have a mild flavour. Where a stronger flavour is needed the dill seeds are used.

Marjoram: A frequently used herb much the same as thyme, although it has a slightly more delicate flavour. Used for meat, egg and vegetable dishes.

Oregano: Related to marjoram but much stronger. Used in Italian dishes. Add it to tomato sauce for pasta, pizza,casseroles and the filling for ravioli.

Parsley: A favourite herb. Usually used fresh on almost any savoury dish.

Rosemary: Spikes of rosemary give a most appetising fragrance to casseroles, soups and many vegetable dishes; a favourite with lamb.

Sage: The broad, flat, crinkled leaves of sage give an unmistakable flavour to meat stuffings.

Savory: The spiky leaves of winter savory taste like a mixture of rosemary and sage. Summer savory is similar but milder. Both go well with bean dishes or in herbed butter.

Spearmint: The most commonly grown mint. Makes excellent mint sauce to serve with lamb and is a welcome addition to salads or peas.

Tarragon: Should be used sparingly. Has a quite unique flavour and aroma and is ideal in bland-flavoured foods such as chicken, mayonnaise and some vegetables.

Thyme: A very familiar herb frequently used with sage in stuffings but similar itself to marjoram. Can be added to vegetables and minced meat dishes.

Note: If dried herbs are used, halve the quantity you would use for fresh herbs. Dried herbs have a much stronger flavour.

Spices

In its pure sense, the word **spice** refers only to parts of aromatic plants grown in the tropics — **true** spices like ginger, pepper, tumeric, cinnamon and mace. But nowadays, for the purpose of buying and cooking, the word has come to include aromatic seeds like anise, fennel and coriander as well as the familiar cinnamon, nutmeg and mixed spice. We add spices now for enjoyment, not to cover up the flavour of bad food as happened in the past when the spice-trading ships carried a very precious cargo across the world.

Spices should be bought in small amounts because they start losing flavour in three to six months, depending on their container. Long exposure to heat, moisture or air should be avoided. In cooking, spices need careful measuring so that they will improve the flavour of the food rather than smother it. With foods that require long cooking, spices are generally added near the end. With uncooked foods they are added well in advance of serving.

Some popular spices

Allspice: Also known as Jamaica pepper, allspice tastes like a blend of cloves, cinnamon and nutmeg. Purchased as berries or ground.

Caraway seeds: Use in cakes and to flavour vegetable dishes, sauces and bread. Have a rather strong flavour. Purchase in seed form.

Cardamom: One of the basic spices used in Indian cooking, and also popular in Scandinavia. The seeds are contained inside the fibrous shell. Can be purchased whole or ground.

Cayenne pepper: A *very* hot pepper, to be used with extreme caution. Ground from a blend of dried chillies. Use sparingly.

Chillies: A variety of red, green and dried Mexican chillies, all from the capsicum family, used in curry powders. Red chilli powder is very hot — use cautiously.

Cinnamon: This comes from the bark of a tree of the laurel family and is available in powdered or stick form. It does not keep its aroma long. Try it with apples, or to flavour fruit cakes and puddings.

Cloves: These are dried flower buds, pungent and spicy, used in stewed fruit, especially apples, and in roast meats, for example, gammon.

Coriander: Seeds and leaves are both used in Middle Eastern cooking and Indian dishes. Has a very delicate 'special' flavour.

Cumin: The powder ground from these seeds, combined with fenugreek, gives commercial curry powder its flavour. Use with pulses (dried peas and beans) or in Middle Eastern meat dishes. Available in seed or powdered form.

Curry powder: Indian cooks always blend their own, varying the proportions of the spices to suit the dish. Usually contains cumin, turmeric, fenugreek and more.

Fennel: Both the dried stalks and the seeds are used in European and Far Eastern cooking. They have a celery-like, aniseed flavour. Could be classed as a herb.

Fenugreek: One of the ingredients used in commercial curry powders. Use very sparingly, the flavour is 'raw' and strong.

Garam masala: Indian cooking depends on this spice mixture. It is a mixture of green cardamoms, cinnamon, cumin plus coriander, cloves and fennel.

Ginger: A powder made from the dried root of the ginger plant. Use a little in casseroles and fruit dishes and for flavouring cakes.

Mace: This is the lacy coating of the nutmeg. Both mace and nutmeg come from the same tropical tree, mace being fuller, stronger and sweeter than the nutmeg it encases. Use in cakes, fruits, with vegetables such as beans and cabbage or sprinkle on baked custard.

Mustard seed: Found in a beige colour, red or dark brown form. Whole mustard seed is not as pungent as when ground; try mixing red and yellow in varying proportions. Hot in flavour, add to salads and meats.

Paprika: A sweet, warm-tasting aromatic red pepper. It losses its flavour if stored for too long. Use it in salad dressings, beaten into curd cheese for filling baked potatoes or with veal. Can be hot or sweet paprika.

Peppercorns: Can be black or white. White peppercorns have the wrinkled black outer layer removed. White pepper is sharper than black. Use white pepper where the black would spoil the appearance of the dish. Best purchased whole and ground fresh.

Saffron: This comes from the orange stigmas of a *mauve crocus*. Buy the filaments to be more sure of getting the genuine article.

Use sparingly to flavour rice. Has little flavour but is a very powerful orange colouring.

Star anise: Used in a great many Asian dishes. Smells and tastes of aniseed. When purchased whole it is removed before serving the dish. Try flavouring black tea with it.

Turmeric: A bright yellow powder ground from the root of the *Curcuma longa* bush. Used in rice dishes or to give an exotic touch to simple vegetable dishes. Gives curry its typical colour.

Workshop

1 Compare as many fresh herbs as possible with their dried counterparts. Compare their aroma and compare them in different dishes. Bring them from home if you have them in the garden.

2 Make a list of the herbs and spices you feel you should use cautiously.

3 Learn about the various spices on the previous pages. Taste them, smell them, use some of them in the ways suggested. Make sure you know about all the spices in the Home Economics Room store.

4 Some spices have uses other than in cooking. See how many of these you can find.

5 Plant a herb garden for your school or home. Use pots or design a garden in a spare piece of ground.

Recipes to Try

Lamb Kebabs

Ingredients

500 g boned lamb cut into 2 cm cubes
1 tsp ginger
2 tsp coriander
1 tsp turmeric
pinch salt
2 tsp yoghurt
30 g safflower oil or melted butter
boiling water

Method

1 Mix all spices with yoghurt.

2 Soak meat in boiling water for 5 mins then remove it and drain well.

3 Place meat and spice mixture in a large bowl and mix well to coat all pieces of meat.

4 Leave to stand for 20 mins, longer if possible.

5 Thread meat on metal skewers.

6 Grill under a pre-heated grill lined with foil. Baste continually with the oil or butter.

7 Turn regularly to allow even cooking. Collect juice caught on foil lining and serve as sauce.

8 Serve with rice.

Serves 4.

Traditional Curry

Ingredients

450 g lean meat eg boned lamb or braising steak
1 carton natural yoghurt (150 g)
3–4 garlic cloves peeled and crushed
20 g fresh ginger root or 1 tsp ground ginger
1 tsp ground coriander
1½ tsps ground cumin
15 g ground almonds
1 tsp garam masala powder
25 g ghee or 2 tbsps oil
 225 g onion peeled and chopped
1 tsp chilli powder

Method

1 Cut meat into bite sized pieces. Put meat, yoghurt, garlic, ginger, coriander, cumin, almonds and garam masala in a bowl. Mix together well, cover and leave to marinade for 1 hour.

2 Heat oil and fry the onion until light brown. Add meat and marinade and fry until browned.

3 Cover and simmer gently for 45 mins to 1 hour until the meat is tender.

4 Add the chilli powder and cook for another 5 mins.

Serve with rice or chappatis.
Serves 4.

Questions about the recipes (Curry and Kebabs)

1 What purpose did each of the spices serve in the recipes?

2 What is the origin of each spice used in these two recipes?

3 Find out about the countries of origin of the two recipes. Why do you think they use lot of spices?

4 What is the purpose in each recipe of allowing the meat to marinate?

Food Puzzles

1 The same letters are missing from each of the 'food words' below. Work out what they are and write the words in your book.
BR___D   ST___K
CR___M   Y___ST
KN___D   F___ST
Write a sentence which includes all six of the words you completed. (You may add 'ed' or 'ing' if you wish.)

2 Unjumble the letters in the puzzle and use them to complete the 'food words' below.

        __ea__
        __ea__
        __ea__
        __ea__
        __ea__
    __ __ ea __ __ __ __
        __ea__
        __ea__

3 If you carefully study the pictures below
you should be able to list ten foods.

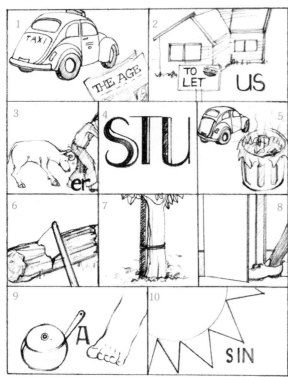

4 **Crossword Clues**

Across

2 Young beef
4 Meat, milk, fish, eggs and cheese
contain this nutrient
6 Soup may be served in one
7 We eat 150 g of this a day
9 Cooks quickly under radiant heat
12 _____tablespoon of fat daily is all you
need
14 Sugar comes from this
15 You do this at meal times

Down

1 _____for children is a
function of the family
2 A nutrient that comes in many forms
3 Meat, milk and butter are_____
foods
5 Have shells and a delicious inside
8 A vegetarian will_____not to eat
meat
10 Carrots, parsnips, turnips and radishes
belong to this classification of
vegetables
11 A cereal
13 A legume or pulse

6 Looking at Food

In order to plan and serve attractive,
appetising meals we not only need to know
about nutrition and cooking but also about the
shape, colour, texture and taste of food.

Investigation No. 19
What Shape is Food?

Aim

- To become aware of the different shapes of the food we eat and how
  some of these shapes can be utilised when preparing food

Procedure

a Draw and label each food you ate at your last evening meal.

b How many different shapes are there?

c Which shapes are *natural* and which shapes are *created* by mixing or
   cutting the food? Write 'natural' or 'created' beside each of your
   drawings. (Activities 'a', 'b' and 'c' can be done for homework.)

d Experiment with ways to utilise the natural shapes of food when
   preparing some dishes.
   Suggested dishes for you to try:
   Jacket potato — you could scoop it out, mash and mix with cheese.
   Stuffed pepper — filled with meat, rice, tomato sauce, herbs, onion
   and baked in the oven.
   Compote of pear — peeled, cooked whole or in half.
   Savoury eggs — hard-boiled yolks mashed with tomato sauce and a
   pinch of curry powder then piled back into eggwhite.
   Banana boat — a cheese sail attached to a whole banana and served in
   a salad.
   Noisettes of lamb.
   Baked apple — cored, scored, filled with dates or raisins, baked in
   ovenproof dish containing 3 tbsp water.
   Fruit salad pineapple — half a pineapple with leaves still attached,
   scooped out and filled with fruit salad.

e Record the type of dishes made and how they look.

f Make up a collection of foods that can be mixed and formed into shapes. Some shapes are made before the food is cooked and some shapes are formed during the cooking process. Suitable recipes follow this Investigation. Discuss and record how the shapes are formed and maintained.

g Comment on each type of recipe made up in class. Discuss results comparing 'before' and 'after' appearances of foods.

h Discuss the types of foods used and when they would be served.

i Think about other food shapes you can make, such as pasties, pies, duchesse potatoes, asparagus rolls, vandyked tomatoes and so on.

Discussion/Conclusion

— How do we make food different shapes?

— How would you react to a meal where everything served had been set into a mould and turned out, for example,

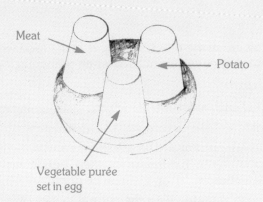

Meat
Potato
Vegetable purée
set in egg

Try this out and note the reactions of others as well as your own feelings.

— Make a list of reasons why it is important to be aware of the shapes of foods and why we serve meals with a variety of shapes.

Chop
Potato
Carrot
Peas

Recipes to Try

Gingerbread Man
(shape made before baking)

Ingredients

150 g plain flour
1 tbsp brown sugar
1 tsp ground ginger
½ tsp cinnamon
30 g margarine
2 tbsp treacle

Method

1 Mix together flour, sugar, ginger and cinnamon as you sift them together.

2 Melt the margarine and treacle and pour over the other mixture.

3 Work the mixture together and knead until smooth.

4 Roll out the mixture on a lightly floured board until it is about ½ cm thick. Cut out with gingerbread man cutter.

5 Lift carefully onto a lightly greased tray. Add currants for eyes, nose and buttons.

6 Bake at 180°C, gas mark 4 for 12 mins.

7 Cool on a wire rack.

Fruit Custards
(Shape made during baking)

Ingredients

3 eggs (size 3)
250 ml skimmed milk
15 g castor sugar
4 teaspoons reduced sugar jam

Method

1 Place 1 teaspoon in jam in each of 4 teacups or greased individual moulds.

2 Make custard. Beat the eggs with the castor sugar, warm the milk until it steams and then stir it into the egg mixture, strain into a jug and pour over the jam, in the teacups.

3 Stand the teacups in a roasting tin with 1 cm of warm water.

4 Bake in oven 160°C, gas mark 3 for 40 minutes until set.

5 To serve, turn out of cups onto serving dishes. Serve hot or cold.

Serves 4.

Corn Bread
(shape made during baking)

Ingredients

150 g cornmeal (polenta)
50 g flour
55 g sugar
½ tbsp baking powder
1 egg
100 g margarine
150 ml milk

Method

1 Sift cornmeal, flour, sugar and baking powder through a coarse sieve.

2 Beat eggs, melt margarine and leave to cool, then stir in the milk.

3 Make a well in the centre of the dry ingredients, add eggs and milk mixture and beat until smooth.

4 Place in a lined, greased 500 g loaf tin.

5 Bake in the centre of a hot oven 220°C, gas mark 7 for 30–45 mins or until the bread is golden brown and has shrunk slightly away from the edges of the tin. Test with a skewer if in doubt.

6 Serve hot in thick slices.

Extra notes on flour mixtures taking shape

What makes your flour mixtures take and hold their shape when baked?

There are three main elements involved:

1 The **heat** of the oven.

2 The sticky elastic protein substance in wheat called **gluten**.

3 A **raising agent**. In the Corn Bread recipe above, the raising agents are baking powder and the air that is trapped as the loaf is mixed. Other raising agents are: yeast; phosphates added to make self-raising flour; mixtures of acid and an alkali, for example, cream of tartar (acid) and bicarbonate of soda (alkali), fruit juice and bicarbonate of soda, dried fruit and bicarbonate of soda, and treacle (contains acid) and bicarbonate of soda.

These three elements work together to form the spongy structure we are familiar with in baked flour mixtures. The heat of the oven causes the gas bubbles (usually carbon dioxide) given off by the raising agent to expand and rise up through the mixture. As the gas bubbles rise, they push the mixture up and stretch the gluten. When the mixture gets hot enough it is set by the heat of the oven.

● Mix an acid and an alkali together to understand more fully how gas is given off (vinegar and bicarbonate of soda give a quick reaction). Imagine this gas pushing up through the sticky flour mixture.

Some raising agents need special care. For example:

● A very light mixture like a sponge cake with lots of air bubbles trapped must be treated very gently before it is baked.

● Any recipes with yeast must be kept very warm all the time before baking (yeast is a micro-organism and needs sugar, warmth and moisture to 'grow', as it grows it gives off carbon dioxide CO_2).

● Any bicarbonate of soda mixtures should be cooked as soon as mixed because they start to work as soon as they get wet, unlike phosphates which don't work until they are heated in the oven.

What Colour Is Food?

Look back at the drawings of foods shapes you did in step (a) of Investigation No. 19. Colour them as closely to their actual colour. How many colours are there? How many colours for the whole class? Why is food so many different colours? List as many reasons as you can.

Workshop

Serve up a number of familiar foods, e.g. spaghetti, mashed potato, custard, stewed apple but colour them with tasteless food colours, e.g. green spaghetti, blue potato, etc. What were your reactions to the appearance? Taste the foods and record your feelings.

Investigation No. 20
Food Colours

Aim

- To become aware of the colour of food and how it can be used when serving food.

Procedure

a The members of the class will be divided into pairs.

b Your teacher will tell those of each pair whether they are person A or person B.

c Person A will work from the instructions in the lefthand column below and person B will work from the instructions in the right hand column below.

d Work carefully, neatly and quickly through your instructions, working with your partner *only* when you need to share equipment and when collecting your ingredients.

e Serve your meal as instructed below.

Person A	Person B
1 Set your table.	1 Set your table.

2 Collect the following ingredients:
    1 piece of carrot
    approximately
    5 cm long
    1 frankfurter
    ½ tomato
    1 small canned beetroot
    2 tsp margarine
	2 Collect the following ingredients:
	    1 small potato
	    2 tbsp canned corn kernels
	    1 frankfurter
	    3 French beans
	    1 tsp margarine

3 Peel carrot and slice into rings ¼–½ cm thick. Place in a small saucepan with water 2 cm deep. Put lid on saucepan and place on cooker. Bring to boil then simmer for 10 mins.	3 Peel potato, cut in half and place in small saucepan with just enough water to cover, add ¼ tsp salt. Put lid on, bring to boil and cook for 15 mins.

Person A	Person B
4 As soon as carrot is on the cooker, place frankfurter in saucepan and cover with warm water (share with partner). Place on cooker and bring to boil then turn down and simmer for 10 mins.	4 Wash beans and cut into 2 cm lenghts. Place on stove and bring to boil in a saucepan with 2 cm water and ¼ tsp salt. Simmer for 10 mins.
5 Light grill. Sprinkle tomato with a little salt and pepper and dot with margarine. Place under grill until just tender (5–10 mins).	5 Place frankfurter in saucepan with your partner's frankfurter, cook as per partner's instructions.
6 Cut beetroot into slices or cubes and sauté gently in 1 tsp margarine.	6 Sauté corn in 1 tsp margarine.
7 Serve all cooked foods together neatly arranged on a white plate.	7 Serve all foods you prepared in a neat manner on a white plate.

f Examine the two served meals. Which one do you think looks the best to eat?

A ☐   or   B ☐   (tick one box)

g Give three reasons for your answer.

h Eat your meal.

i Clean the Home Economics Room.

j Each pupil should now fill in the following table without consulting their partner or any other pupil in the class.

	Excellent (score 9)	Very Good (score 8)	Good (score 7)	Satisfactory (score 6)	Average (score 5)	Fair (score 4)	Poor (score 3)	Very poor (score 2)	Unacceptable (score 1)
Meal A Appearance									
Odour									
Taste*									
Meal B Appearance									
Odour									
Taste*									

*You can only score for the meal you ate.

k Compare your answers with those of your partner.

l Compare your answers with those of the rest of the class. Your teacher will help here by compiling the total scores of the class on the board.

m What decisions can you make about how to use colour when serving food?

How Does Food Taste?

We taste our food with our tongues. The tongue, as you know, is a very important part of your mouth. The tongue is made of muscle that moves freely. It also contains lots of nerve endings (remember how it hurts when you bite your tongue or when you drink a cup of tea that is too hot?).

We use our tongues, not only to taste our food, but also to talk, to keep food moving while we are chewing and to help us to swallow.

The taste of food can give us pleasure as we enjoy eating our favourite foods, or let us know when we find something unpleasant.

There are probably about 9000 taste buds on the tongue. We have four main tastes: **sweet, bitter, sour, salty**. All other tastes are mixtures of these four.

The taste buds which make us experience taste are on the upper part of the tongue's surface, and we taste the four main tastes on different areas of our tongue. The diagram below will help you to understand this.

When planning meals we enjoy using flavours that complement each other, such as the sweet/sour flavour of the pork recipe (see page 158) combined with the bland flavour of the boiled rice.

Investigation No. 21 should help you to understand taste more fully.

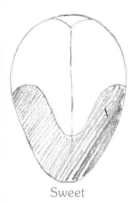
Sweet

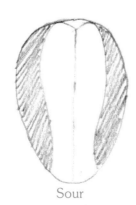
Sour

Bitter

Salty

Investigation No. 21
Food Tasting

Aim
- To discover how people identify the taste of food.

Procedure

a The name of a taste appears in each of six circles below. Copy these into your book and write the names of at least three foods in each circle that you think belong with the taste.

b Play the following tasting game:
   — Prepare six small plates of food cut very small.
   — Three pupils volunteer to be the *tasters*. They are blindfolded. (They should not have been involved in preparing the food).
   — The teacher then places signs on the foods to reveal the food type to the rest of the class.
   — Each taster will be fed a teaspoon of each food, and tells the class what the food is. The class must be very quiet so that the taster does not know whether s/he is right or wrong.
   — Tasters should not be fed the foods in the same order.
   For example,
   Taster 1: Taste Food 1 then 2,3,4,5,6
   Taster 2: Taste Food 3 then 1,5,2,4,6
   Taster 3: Taste Food 6 then 3,1,5,4,2

— The class will record the results in a table like the one below.

Name of food (examples)	Food 1 mashed potato	Food 2 stewed apple	Food 3 grated carrot	Food 4 diced tomato	Food 5 mashed banana	Food 6 meat sauce
Taster 1						
Taster 2						
Taster 3						

(Tick if taster gets the food correct. If wrong, write in the answer given.)
— Three more volunteer tasters will undertake the following activity:

- Your teacher will have six more plates of food prepared but this time will not reveal to anyone what these foods are.
- Tasters are not blindfolded this time and each taster tastes each food in turn and writes his or her answers without revealing them until the tasting is finished.
- Tasters will read out their results to the class and the class will fill in a table like the one below.

	Food 1	Food 2	Food 3	Food 4	Food 5	Food 6
Taster 1						
Taster 2						
Taster 3						

(Write in the answers given by the tasters.)
Name of food: (revealed by teacher after table is filled)

Discussion/Conclusion

c Look at the results of both tastings. In what ways are they different? Write an analysis and conclusion of the results.

You have learnt that the tongue is the part of the body that enables us to taste. You learnt in Investigations No. 19 and 20 that the way food looks influences what we eat or how we feel about food Do you think that our eyes have anything to do with our ability to identify the foods? In other words do you think we *eat with our eyes?*

From the last three practical exercises you can see that when planning meals it is important to be aware of the shape of food, to use colours that please and a mixture of flavours that please. We also have become aware that different people like and dislike different foods, and this must be considered when preparing food for others.

Recipes to Try

Sweet and Sour Pork

Ingredients

600 g lean pork
1 tsp sugar
1½ tbsp soy sauce
1 tbsp dry sherry or red wine vinegar
1 egg yolk
cornflour
oil for deep frying
1 small onion
4 spring onions
½ red pepper
60 g mushrooms
½ cucumber
1 stick celery
1½ tbsp oil, extra
470 g pineapple pieces
2 tbsp tomato ketchup
60 ml white vinegar
250 ml water
1 chicken stock cube
1 tbsp extra cornflour

Method

1 Combine sugar, 1½ tbsp soy sauce, sherry and egg yolk, stir well.

2 Cut meat into 2½ cm dice, place into soy sauce mixture, stir until meat is evenly coated. Cover and leave for ¾ hour, stir occasionally (this is a marinade).

3 Drain meat from marinade, keep liquid.

4 Toss meat lightly in cornflour. Heat oil and cook meat until golden brown and cooked through, about 7 mins. Do this in several batches so meat browns well and pieces remain separate. Drain on absorbent paper.

5 Peel and slice onion, slice spring onions diagonally, slice pepper thickly, slice mushrooms and celery, cut cucumber into quarters lengthwise, remove seeds then slice.

6 Heat oil in pan or wok, add all the vegetables and sauté for 3 mins.

7 Drain pineapple and add pineapple syrup to pan with marinade from meat, also remaining soy sauce, tomato sauce, vinegar and crumbled stock cube.

8 Blend extra cornflour and water, add to pan, stir until sauce thickens.

9 Add pineapple pieces, season with salt and pepper if necessary. Add pork, stir until combined.

Serves 4.

Chicken Marengo

Ingredients

2 chicken portions
salt
freshly ground pepper
1 tbsp oil
1 clove garlic, finely chopped
125 g mushrooms, sliced
400 g can peeled tomatoes
1 chicken stock cube
2 tbsp tomato purée
boiled rice for serving
parsley and paprika for garnish

Method

1 Remove skin from chicken portions.

2 Heat oil and sauté chicken till golden brown, add garlic and mushrooms, sauté 2 mins. Add tomato juice from can, stock cube, tomato purée and pepper to taste.

3 Place in casserole dish. Cook in oven at 190°C, gas mark 5 for 45 mins.

4 Serve with boiled rice. Garnish with parsley and paprika.

Serves 2.

Crisp Fried Vegetables

Ingredients

2 tbsp oil
¼ small cabbage, shredded
1 stick celery, sliced
125 g carrots, sliced
125 g beans, sliced
125 g mushrooms, sliced
1 tbsp ginger root, finely chopped
freshly ground pepper
2 tbsp soy sauce

Serves 4.

Method

Heat oil. Add vegetables, ginger and pepper. Fry for 2 mins. Add soy sauce. Simmer for 3 mins. Serve.

Crazy Puzzle

This crossword is not difficult, but the clues are a bit crazy! All answers to the clues are food items.

Number 3 across has been filled in to give you some idea of how to complete the puzzle. The clue tells us that someone buries something — the food answer is therefore berries!

CLUES

ACROSS:

2.

3.

5.

7.

9.

11.

14.

15.

DOWN:

1.

4.

5.

6.

8.

10.

12.

13.

Questions to answer

Select any one of the foods in the puzzle and write as much as you can about it. For example, where it comes from (farm, market garden, factory), what shape it is, what colour it is inside and out, how it is prepared, and the nutritive value it has. Use this book and others to help you.

What is it?

(This activity incorporates areas up to and including this chapter.)

a It is something you use to achieve your goals. It can be human or non-human.

b It influences everything you do. It is fairly well established in early childhood and does not change much, but it might change in the way it is expressed.

c It should occur after any decision has been managed or after any task has been completed. It helps you to see where improvements might be made or to help you to feel satisfied.

d It is used to help in the improvement of the management of time and energy. Pathways are plotted on it, examined, and decisions are made about how a process might be improved.

e It is the first part of the decision-making process. It can be pleasant or unpleasant, simple or complex.

f Unless it is understood by others it is of little use. It can involve sound, signs or movement.

g It is a group of people living together. They may be of different ages and may be different sexes. It often has two adults but might only have one.

h It is probably the most important resource to have. To function well it must be accepted by others and communicate effectively.

i Without it the human body cannot function. It comes in all shapes, sizes, textures, colours and flavours. Every cell in the body needs this.

j It saves energy by use of a fan to move hot air in an enclosed space. It cooks food evenly and efficiently.

7 Finding Out About Meals

Purchasing Food

The purchasing of food for a family or an individual is an exercise in management.

What are some possible goals a person or family may have when making their food purchases?

What resources are involved in the planning and purchasing of food?

Which of these resources can be used only once? Which can be used several times?

Many decisions have to be made while planning and shopping. What factors will influence the decisions a person makes while shopping for food?

Foods can be purchased in many different forms. For example, peas can be purchased dried (split peas), canned, frozen or fresh. When shopping for family meals decisions will be made relating to the form in which food will be purchased. Such decisions will be influenced by:

- what is available
- cost
- storage space and type
- skills of caterer
- family preferences
- function in recipe, for example, split peas make better pea soup than fresh peas but fresh peas are preferable to serve as a vegetable.

Workshop

1 a From the recipes at the end of this workshop plan a dinner menu for a family of four.

 b Prepare a food shopping list including the quantity and form of each food needed. Indicate where you will buy each food — at the green grocer, butcher, supermarket, fishmonger, etc. These shopping lists are called 'food orders'. Before preparing your list, take note that the following ingredients are available in the store cupboard: plain flour, self-raising white flour, wholemeal flour, margarine, frying oil, salt, pepper, a range of spices and herbs, tomato sauce, Worcestershire sauce, soya sauce, sugar, rice and six onions.

 c If possible, prepare the menu. Did you remember to order all the ingredients? Were there some ingredients that were not available? If so, what, if anything, did you substitute?

2 What are three different forms in which each of the following foods can be purchased? Carrots, sausages, tomato paste.

3 A can of tomato soup costs 51p and will serve four people. Calculate the cost per serving to the nearest penny.

4 Three advertisements for orange juice are shown below. Which orange juice is the least expensive per litre?

30p

SPECIAL!

95p   £1.69p

5 a Pictures of foods in various forms are shown on the opposite page. Select the most appropriate form of food for each of the situations suggested. Give at least one reason for each decision you make.

 Select the best choice of potato for:
 • a hiking trip
 • potato salad
 • roasting with a leg of lamb
 • a snack at the football match.

Select the best choice of hamburgers for:
- dinner for a low-income family
- a barbecue for fifty people
- the most nutritious meal from the alternatives.

Fresh
minced meat

Frozen
hamburgers

Take-away hamburger

Ready-made
hamburger from butcher
uncooked

b Were the answers from the whole class to the above the same? Discuss the possible reasons for any differences.

5 a List four of your favourite vegetables and four of your favourite fruits. Can you buy these all the year round? When are your favourites in season in the area where you live? (See pages 109–111 and 120–122 for help.)

b How are we able to buy fresh plant foods when they are out of season?

c Find out the cost per kilogram of your favourites. Repeat the exercise a week later. Were the prices different from one week to the next? Why?

Recipes to Try

Fish or Meat Spirals

Fish Ingredients

30 g margarine
30 g flour
shake of pepper
250 ml milk
425 g can mackerel, drained, bones removed
1 tsp chopped parsley
½ grated onion
juice and finely grated rind of ½ lemon

Method

1 Melt the margarine, add flour and pepper and cook for 1 min, stirring continually. This is a roux.
2 Add milk, stir continually until the mixture thickens and boils.
3 Remove from the stove and stir in all the other ingredients.
4 Pour into a casserole *or* divide into 4 ramekins.
5 Top with Spiral Mixture (below).

Meat Ingredients

400 g minced steak
½ onion
250 ml water
1 beef stock cube
2 tsp flour
2 tsp tomato purée
1 tsp soy sauce

Method

1 Dice onion finely.
2 Crumble beef stock cube into water.
3 Put all ingredients into saucepan and mix well with a wooden spoon.
4 Put on cooker, stir occasionally until boiling, simmer for 15 mins.
5 Pour into a casserole *or* divide into 4 ramekins.
Then make one quantity of:

Spiral Mixture Ingredients

100 g S.R. flour
50 g S.R. wholemeal flour
50 g margarine
2 tbsp cheese spread *or* 25 g grated cheese
3 tbsp milk
1 slice cooked ham
pinch cayenne pepper
1 small carrot grated

Method

1 Sift flours and cayenne pepper. Add bran back into sifted flour.
2 Rub margarine into flour.
3 Mix to a firm dough with milk.
4 Knead lightly and roll into a rectangle 1 cm thick.
5 Spread with cheese spread or sprinkle with grated cheese. Sprinkle with carrot and chopped ham, leaving a margin around the edge.

6 Roll up like a swiss roll, moisten one end to stick.
7 Cut into 8 slices 2–3 cm thick.

8 Place on top of mixture in casserole, spiral side facing upwards.

9 Bake at 200°C, gas mark 6 for 30 mins.
Serves 4.

Note The spiral mixture may be used on its own to make a savoury snack for packed lunches. Cook spirals on a greased baking tray for 15 mins 220°C, gas mark 7.

Israeli Beef Pancakes

Ingredients

2 medium potatoes, cooked and mashed
1 small onion, grated
3 beaten eggs
1/2 tsp paprika
1/4 tsp black pepper
250 g cold cooked beef, minced or cut into fine dice
1 tbsp finely chopped parsley
2 tbsp oil

Method

1 Combine potato, onion, eggs, pepper, beef and parsley and mix well. Heat oil in frying pan.

2 Pour egg mixture into pan, 1 cup at a time. Cook slowly until firm enough to turn over.

3 Cook on other side for 2 mins.

4 Sprinkle with paprika and serve.
Serves 4.

Mixed Grill Kebabs

Ingredients

300 g lean pork or lamb
4 rashers bacon
6 thin pork sausages

Method

1 Cut meat into cubes of approximately 2 cm, cut sausages into 2 cm pieces, cut bacon into 10 cm lengths and make into rolls.

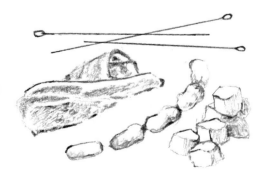

2 Thread meat, sausages and bacon alternately onto skewers.

3 Place under grill turning often to cook the meat evenly. Cook for 20–30 mins.

Serve with rice and Piquant Tomatoes p. 31
Serves 4.

Green Salad

Ingredients

2 sticks celery
1/4 lettuce
1/2 green pepper
1/4 cucumber
50 g sultanas

Method

1 Wash lettuce, soak in cold water until crisp. Tear into smallish pieces.

2 Chop celery.

3 Remove seeds from pepper and chop.

4 Dice cucumber.

5 Toss prepared vegetables with sultanas and add a little Tasty Dressing (see recipe on the next page).
Serves 4.

Tasty Salad Dressing

Ingredients

3 tbsp lemon juice
½ tbsp honey
pinch garlic salt
pinch celery salt
½ tomato
½ tsp paprika
1 tsp peanut butter
125 ml vegetable oil

Method

1 Combine all ingredients, except oil, in blender. Blend thoroughly.

2 Slowly blend in oil.
Keeps for a week or so in the refrigerator.

Minted Peas

Ingredients

500 g peas
250 ml water
a little mint
1 tsp butter

Method

1 Shell peas.

2 Boil water, add peas and mint.

3 Boil 10–15 mins or until tender. Drain and toss in butter.

Serves 4.

Devilled Carrots

Ingredients

350 g carrot
50 g margarine
1 tbsp brown sugar
½ tsp mustard
1 tbsp water

Method

1 Peel and wash carrots.

2 Cut into sticks 6 cm × 5 mm.

3 Sauté in melted margarine for 5 mins, then add sugar, mustard and water.

4 Simmer 10 mins.

Serves 4.

Creamed Rice Dessert

Ingredients

100 g short grain rice
250 ml water
500 ml milk
2 tbsp sugar

Method

1 Cook rice in water until water is absorbed.

2 Add milk and cook until thick. Stir occasionally to prevent sticking.

3 Mix in sugar and pour into wetted moulds.

4 When set turn out of moulds on to serving plate. If time is short serve directly into dessert bowls.

Serves 4.

Cheesecake

Ingredients

75 g digestive biscuits
50 g margarine, melted
250 g cottage cheese or low-fat cream cheese
150 ml double cream
50 g caster sugar
Grated rind and juice of 1 lemon.
Fresh or tinned fruit.

Method

1 Crush biscuits. Mix with melted margarine and press on to the base of an 18 cm flan dish. Chill.

2 Make cottage cheese smooth by rubbing through a sieve. Whip cream until thick.

3 Fold cottage cheese, sugar, lemon rind and juice into cream.

4 Spread mixture over crumbs.

5 Decorate with fruit.

Planning the Menu

Although nutritional value should be the basis for meal planning, other goals may be achieved such as attractiveness of colour and shape, as well as appetising flavour and pleasing texture combinations.

The type of meals served will be influenced by the age, state of health, occupation, activities and food likes and dislikes of the individual, food cost in relation to money available, food available (season, local market, home-produced, home-preserved and the ability to use leftovers), equipment for cooking, time available for preparation, ability and experience in food preparation, and the occasion at which the meal is to be served.

A Guide to Breakfast

Breakfast should be quick to prepare. Foods from the 'Eat Most' group should be used to fuel the body for a good start to the day. The 'Eat Moderately' group should be represented also to give protein and a balance of all vitamins.

Breakfast is a *must* to fuel the body after a long rest.

A Guide to Lunch

All of the Healthy Diet Pyramid should be represented in proportion although sugar should be omitted if you are not able to clean your teeth. Plenty of fruit and vegetables should be eaten at this meal to assist digestion and add fibre to the diet.

Make it appetising.

A Guide to Packed Lunches

Many people take a packed meal to school or work for lunchtime. Packed meals often contain high fat and sugar foods such as crisps, chocolate, cakes, biscuits, fizzy drinks. With a little thought healthy packed meals can be planned which follow the healthy eating guidelines.

A Guide to Evening Meal

This is usually the largest meal, any sugar you wish to include could be part of this meal but only a very small amount.

Protein, carbohydrate and vitamin B foods must be included.

Serve it neatly and attractively.

Planning menus in advance usually leads to greater economy of time, energy and money and is more likely to result in meals which represent the Healthy Diet Pyramid (see page 86) in the desired balance of foods as well as those which apply the Dietary Guidelines (see page 87).

Workshop

1 Draw together all you have learnt in your lessons on nutrition with the information in the last three sections relating to the colour, shape and taste of food, and plan a two-course dinner for your family. Explain the reason for the inclusion of each food.

2 In pairs or a group of four, apply your knowledge of the nutrition, colour, shape and taste of food and plan an evening meal from the recipes at the end of this workshop and elsewhere in this book (use **recipe index** on page 198 to help you). Multiply or divide the recipes as necessary then write out a food order for the foods required.
Prepare your meal.
Repeat this exercise for:
— a breakfast menu for an adolescent
— a packed lunch for a bricklayer
— Saturday lunch for the family.

Evaluate **each** of your menus after it has been prepared. In your evaluation consider colour, shape, texture, flavour, attractiveness and the nutritional value of the meal.

3 Plan a low cost menu for a day for a family which consists of two parents, a ten-year-old girl and a fourteen-year-old boy. The father is unemployed. To do this exercise well you need to know the following:
— The cost of an average daily menu (survey your class) so you can understand what a lower-than-average cost is.
— The average proportion of income available for food.
— The nutritional needs of the relevant age groups represented in this family (see pages 91–95).

4 **Food Puzzle**
There are sixteen foods of various kinds in the puzzle below. Find them all then investigate the nutritive value of each.

Recipes To Try

Breakfast

Fruity Porridge
Ingredients

100 g rolled oats
1 Granny Smith apple

1 tbsp sultanas
1 litre water or milk

Method

1 Simmer together the water and the oats for about 5 mins or until thick.
2 Grate apple and add to the thickened oats with the sultanas. Simmer for a further 5 mins.
Serves 4.

Toasted Savoury Crumpets
Ingredients

4 crumpets
1 egg
2 tbsp milk
100 g grated cheese
2 bacon rashers

Method

1 Toast crumpets lightly on each side.
2 Beat the egg with milk and cheese.
3 Spread each crumpet thickly with mixture and place under grill until just bubbling.
4 Top with half a bacon rasher and return to grill until the bacon is cooked to suit your taste.
Serves 2–4 depending on appetite.

Hawaiian Snack
Ingredients

1 slice wholemeal bread
1 slice ham
1 tsp butter
1 slice pineapple, tinned
1 tbsp grated cheese
a little mustard, if desired

Method

1 Toast bread.

2 Spread toast with butter which has been mixed with a little mustard.

3 Place ham then pineapple on bread, heat under grill. Top with cheese and brown under grill.

Serves 1.

Mexican Scramble

Ingredients

1 large chopped onion
1 chopped green pepper
20 g margarine
1 tsp paprika
100 g grated cheddar cheese
1 small can tomatoes
3 beaten eggs
4 slices buttered toast

Method

1 Cook onion and green pepper in margarine until soft.

2 Add drained tomatoes and simmer for 5 mins.

3 Add paprika and grated cheese. Stir until cheese melts.

4 Mix a small amount of the hot mixture with the beaten eggs, mix all together and cook until thick and creamy.

5 Serve on hot buttered toast.

Serves 4.

Cheese Omelette

Ingredients

2 eggs
25 g grated cheese
15 g margarine

Method

1 Beat eggs lightly to just mix them.

2 Heat margarine in an omelette pan. Pour eggs in and let them cook for a few mins over a gentle heat.

3 Tilt the pan and lift the omelette at one edge with a spatula to allow uncooked mixture to run underneath. Repeat this action 2 or 3 times until all egg is set but still quite wet-looking on top.

4 Sprinkle with cheese and fold in half immediately.

Serves 1.

Lunch

(Note: Some of the breakfast recipes above are suitable for lunch.)

Hot Chicken Salad Sandwich

Ingredients

100 g cold cooked chicken, diced
100 g chopped celery
100 g chopped walnuts (optional)
1 tbsp lemon juice
1 tbsp chopped onion
4 tbsp mayonnaise
4 slices wholemeal bread
½ pkt potato crisps crushed

Method

1 Combine chicken, celery, nuts, lemon juice, mayonnaise.

2 Toast bread on one side. Spread with chicken mixture on untoasted side. Top with crushed crisps. Bake at 220°C, gas mark 7 for 12 mins.

Serves 4.

French Onion Tart

Ingredients

50 g margarine
100 g plain wholemeal flour
1 tbsp water
20 g margarine
1 medium sized cooking onion
2 eggs
100 ml cream or low-fat yoghurt
50 g grated cheese

Method

1 Rub the margarine into the flour until it resembles breadcrumbs.

2 Mix to a firm dough with water.

3 Knead the dough a little until smooth.

4 Roll the dough to line an 18 cm pie plate or flan ring; trim edges. Chill.

5 Slice onions finely and place in a saucepan with the melted margarine. Sprinkle with a little salt and pepper. Cover and sauté for 10 mins.

6 Beat eggs, add cream and onions then pour mixture into pastry shell. Sprinkle with cheese and bake in a hot oven 200°C, gas mark 6 for 30 mins until set and golden brown.

Serves 4–6, keeps for a few days after cooking, and when cold can be sliced for a packed lunch.

Salmon Foo Yung

Ingredients

4 eggs
1 tbsp grated onion
240 g can salmon
2 shakes pepper
pinch garlic powder
1 tbsp oil

Sauce

1 tsp cornflour or arrowroot
1 tsp sugar
1 tsp vinegar
½ chicken cube stock mixed with 60 ml water

Method

1 Beat eggs well, add other non-sauce ingredients except oil and mix lightly.

2 Heat oil in a large pan. Add mixture to pan, one tablespoon at a time; fry until brown, turn each patty to brown on both sides.

3 Serve with Foo Yung sauce made as follows: Combine all sauce ingredients in a small saucepan and stir over a gentle heat until it boils.

Oat Cookies

Ingredients

50 g wholemeal flour
2 tsp baking powder
50 g porridge oats
50 g brown sugar
50 g margarine
1 tbsp skimmed milk

Method

1 Put flour in mixing bowl, stir in baking powder.

2 Add oats, sugar and margarine.

3 Rub all ingredients together to make a crumbly mixture.

4 Add enough milk to make a firm dough.

5 Divide dough into 12 pieces, roll each piece of dough into a ball. Place on a greased baking tray and flatten. Bake in oven at 180°C, gas mark 4.

6 Bake until golden brown.

Greek Salad

Ingredients

1 small red pepper
1 small green pepper
1 large onion
2 ripe tomatoes
2 sticks celery
1 cucumber
125 g black olives
1 small lettuce
60 ml French dressing made with olive oil
125 g feta cheese

Method

1 Slice peppers and remove any seeds.

2 Peel onion, cut into wedges and separate into pieces.

3 Cut tomatoes into wedges, slice celery and dice cucumber.

4 Wash lettuce and tear into pieces.

5 Put all prepared vegetables into a salad bowl. Add olives, cover and refrigerate until ready to serve.

6 Add dressing and toss well, top with diced feta cheese.

Serves 6.

Norway Sardine Bake

Ingredients

100 g spaghetti
124 g can sardines
1 tbsp oil from sardines
50 g grated cheddar cheese
1 large stalk celery
1 small onion
1 chopped peeled tomato
25 g grated tasty cheese

Method

1 Cook spaghetti for 15–20 mins in plenty of boiling, salted water. Drain.

2 Chop vegetables and fry in oil until just tender. Season with a little salt and pepper.

3 Mix vegetables and cheddar cheese with drained spaghetti.

4 Place in greased casserole and cover with sardines. Top with tasty cheese and bake at 200°C, gas mark 6 for 20 mins.

Serves 2–3.

Cheese Biscuits

(Good for short lessons.)

Ingredients

75 g plain flour
1 tbsp S.R. flour
pinch cayenne pepper
50 g margarine
1½ tbsp parmesan cheese
50 g grated cheddar cheese
½ tbsp lemon juice

Method

1 Sift dry ingredients

2 Rub in margarine and grated cheeses.

3 Mix to a firm dough with juice.

4 Shape into a roll 15 cm long and wrap in greaseproof paper then foil. Refrigerate at least 3 hours or overnight (or simply until your next lesson—or it can be frozen if desired).

5 Cut roll into 5 mm slices and place on greased oven trays. Bake at 180°C, gas mark 4 for 15 mins until light golden brown. Cool on a cooling rack.

Makes about 10.

Carrot-Banana Cake

Ingredients

100 g margarine
150 g raw cane sugar
grated rind 1 lemon
1 egg
2 ripe bananas, mashed well
225 g S.R. flour
1 medium sized grated carrot
3 tbsp milk

Method

1 Beat together margarine, sugar and lemon rind until creamy, add egg and beat in with the mashed bananas.

2 Sift flour, add carrot and beat in.

3 Mix to a soft consistency with the milk.

4 Turn into a greased loaf tin 20 cm × 10 cm and bake at 180°C, gas mark 4 for 45–50 mins.

5 Cool in tin.

Packed Lunches

Suggestions for healthy packed meals:

2 crusty brown rolls with low-fat spread and a filling of ham and tomato
2 oat biscuits
1 banana
low calorie orange squash

Egg and cress sandwiches made with wholemeal bread
50 g unsalted peanuts
fruit scone
apple
unsweetened fruit juice

2 chicken drum sticks
1 wholemeal roll
1 carton fruit yoghurt
low calorie fruit squash

Wholemeal crispbreads with cheese or liver pâté filling
1 raw carrot and 1 stick of celery
nuts and raisins
fruit juice

Wholemeal rolls with cheese and tomato
1 slice of carrot banana cake
apple
fruit juice

Cheese scones or spirals
1 tomato
1 carton fruit yoghurt
orange squash

1 slice French onion tart
finger salad of cucumber, tomato and celery chunks
1 carton fruit yoghurt
1 apple
fruit juice

Evening Meal

(Note: Some of the lunch recipes can be used here.)

Main Courses

Gourmet Pork and Rice

Ingredients

450 g pork steak
1 large onion
1 carrot
2 stalks celery
1 tbsp oil
1 green pepper
2 chicken stock cubes
200 g uncooked rice
125 ml pineapple juice
2 tsp chopped parsley
½ tsp paprika

Method

1 Dice pork, onion, carrot, celery and pepper.

2 Fry gently in oil until tender — about 30 mins (put lid on after first 5 mins).

3 ¾ fill a medium saucepan with water and bring to the boil. Add rice and simmer for 12–15 mins. Drain.

4 Mix pork and rice, crumble cubes over mixture and pour in juice. Stir until juice is absorbed.

5 Serve sprinkled with chopped parsley and paprika.

Serves 4.

Mexican Spaghetti

Ingredients

2 tbsp oil
1 clove garlic
2 onions
1 green pepper
400 g minced steak
1 tsp chilli powder
2 tbsp chopped parsley
200 g spaghetti
1 tsp basil
1 large tin tomatoes (400 g)
3 tbsp red wine vinegar

1 beef stock cube
2 tbsp tomato paste
30 g margarine
1 small can kidney beans (220 g)

Method

1 Heat oil, add crushed garlic, peeled and finely chopped onions and chopped pepper. Sauté until onion is transparent.

2 Add meat and brown well.

3 Add chilli and basil, cook 1 min.

4 Add tomatoes with liquid from can, vinegar, cube and tomato paste.

5 Cover and simmer 45 mins adding a little water if mixture becomes dry.

6 Cook spaghetti in a large pan of boiling water until tender, 15–20 mins, drain well. Arrange on serving plates.

7 Heat margarine in pan, sauté drained and rinsed beans for 1 min, stir in parsley.

8 Spoon meat sauce over spaghetti and garnish with beans.

Serves 4.
(To make this for a vegetarian replace meat by doubling the quantity of all vegetables.)

Lemon Chicken

Ingredients

4 chicken breasts
50 g cornflour
3 tbsp water
4 egg yolks
6 spring onions, chopped
oil for deep frying

Sauce

3 tbsp rice flour
50 g sugar
500 ml water
150 ml lemon juice (juice of 1 lemon)
1 chicken stock cube
1 tsp soy sauce
1 tsp grated fresh root ginger

Method

1 Cut each chicken breast into 2 pieces.

2 Make batter by blending cornflour, water and yolks.

3 Dip chicken pieces into cornflour batter and deep fry for 15 mins until cooked through. Drain on absorbent paper. Keep warm.

4 Put rice flour and sugar in saucepan and blend with water and juice. Heat, stirring continually until boiling.

5 Add crumbled cube and all other ingredients, simmer for 3 mins.

6 Slice each cooked chicken piece into 3 or 4 pieces. Serve on warm plate with sauce poured over.

7 Garnish with chopped spring onions.

Serves 4–6.

Vegetables

Ratatouille

Ingredients

½ large aubergine
1 red pepper
1 green pepper
1 courgette
salt and pepper
1 onion
1 clove garlic, crushed
30 ml oil
¼ tsp thyme
2 large tomatoes

Method

1 Peel aubergine, cut into 2.5 cm cubes.

2 Remove seeds from peppers and cut into 2.5 cm squares.

3 Slice courgette and peel and chop onions.

4 Heat 1 tbsp of oil in a pan, add onions, garlic and thyme.

5 Cook until onions are transparent, remove from pan.

6 Sauté each of the vegetables separately in remaining oil.

7 Peel tomatoes, chop roughly, add to vegetables.

8 Add onion to vegetables, season with salt and pepper and bring to boil, reduce heat, simmer uncovered for 10–15 mins.

Serves 4.

Stuffed Courgettes

Ingredients

4 small courgettes
½ tbsp margarine
2 spring onions, chopped
4 tbsp (½ slice bread) bread crumbs.
1 egg yolk
pinch pepper
2 tbsp plain yoghurt
50 g grated cheese
2 tsp chopped parsley

Method

1 Wash courgettes and cut off ends.

2 Cook whole in boiling water with ½ tsp salt for 8–10 mins.

3 Cut a 2.5 cm strip from one end to the other of each courgette. Using a teaspoon carefully scoop out centres—chop this flesh into small pieces.

4 Heat the margarine and sauté the onion till tender. Add chopped courgette centres and cook for 5 mins.

5 Add crumbs, egg, pepper, half the cheese and parsley. Pile mixture into courgette shells.

6 Mix yoghurt and other half of cheese and spread over filling.

7 Bake uncovered at 180°C, gas mark 4 for 30 mins.

Serves 4.

Colcannon

Ingredients

450 g sliced potatoes
225 g shredded cabbage
125 g thinly sliced onion
1 tbsp vegetable oil
salt and freshly ground pepper
30 g butter or margarine

Method

1 Cook potatoes in boiling water for 5–10 mins, or until they can just be pierced with a fork.

2 Put cabbage in a saucepan with about 10 cm water, bring to boil, then drain immediately.

3 Fry onion in oil until golden brown.

4 Add cabbage and continue frying until it is also beginning to brown; sprinkle with salt and pepper and keep hot.

5 Fry par-boiled potatoes in butter until brown and crisp. Add to cabbage and serve at once.

Serves 4.

Fennel with Orange Sauce

Ingredients

2–4 heads fennel (450 g altogether)
20 g margarine
2 tsp wholemeal flour
100 ml orange juice
grated rind of 2 oranges
1–2 tbsp chopped parsley

Method

1 Trim fennel and cut heads into quarters.

2 Cook in boiling water for 10–15 mins.

3 Melt margarine in saucepan, add flour and stir until thick (roux). Blend in the orange juice gradually and stir over gentle heat until sauce boils and thickens.

4 Remove saucepan from cooker and add the orange rind and most of the parsley. Keep warm.

5 Drain fennel and arrange pieces cut sides uppermost. Spoon sauce over, opening the leaves of the fennel to allow sauce to penetrate.

6 Sprinkle with remaining parsley.

Serves 4.

Sweet and Sour Beans

Ingredients

450 g fresh or frozen green beans
20 g margarine
50 g chopped onion
4 tbsp cider vinegar
1 tbsp raw brown sugar
6 large mint leaves chopped very finely

Method

1 Cook fresh beans in a very little boiling, salted water for 10–15 mins or until they are just tender (if using frozen beans, cook according to instructions on packet).

2 Melt margarine in a saucepan, add onion and vinegar and cook for 5 mins.

3 When beans are tender, there should be little or no water left (drain frozen beans, if necessary). Add the sugar, stir until the beans are evenly coated, then add the onion.

4 Stir in the mint and continue stirring gently until onion and mint are thoroughly mixed into the beans.

Serves 4.

Heaven and Earth

Ingredients

350 g diced potatoes
450 g cooking apples
225 g thinly sliced onions
½ tsp cinnamon
2 tbsp oil

Method

1 Cook potatoes in water for about 10 mins — they should still be firm.

2 Peel and dice apples and add them to potatoes after potatoes have been cooking for 7 mins — the apples should cook until tender but not squashy.

3 Fry onions in a pan with cinnamon and half the oil until they are golden brown.

4 Remove onions and keep them hot.

5 Wipe out pan, return it to heat and add the rest of the oil.

6 Drain potatoes and apple, pat dry with paper towel then put them into the hot oil.

7 Fry until beginning to brown, turning them gently.

8 Serve with the onions sprinkled on top.

Serves 4.

Desserts

Rhubarb and Apple Crumble

Ingredients

250 g rhubarb
1 cooking apple
2 tbsp sugar
2 tbsp water

Topping

25 g cornflakes
1 tbsp coconut
1 tbsp brown sugar
2 tbsp condensed or evaporated milk

Method

1 Wash and trim rhubarb, cut into 3 cm pieces.

2 Peel and core apple, cut into quarters and then into thin slices.

3 Put rhubarb and apple in saucepan with water and sugar. Simmer with lid on for 10–14 mins until cooked or cook in a casserole dish in a microwave oven for 5 mins.

4 Put fruit in a casserole.

5 Crush cornflakes then combine all topping ingredients evenly.

6 Put topping over fruit. Bake at 180°C, gas mark 4 for 15 mins or until golden brown.

Serves 4.

Custard Tarts

Pastry Ingredients

100 g plain flour
50 g margarine
4–6 tsp cold water

Custard Ingredients

2 eggs
1 level tbsp sugar
250 ml milk
nutmeg

Method

1 Sift flour and rub in margarine until mixture resembles breadcrumbs.

2 Mix in cold water to form a firm dough. Knead lightly.

3 Roll out to 3 mm thickness and cut with an 8 cm fluted cutter. Put into greased patty tins, gently pushing into shape of tins.

4 Beat all custard ingredients together and pour into a jug.

5 Pour custard carefully into prepared cases filling them to the top. Sprinkle with nutmeg.

6 Carefully, without spilling, put into an oven on 200°C, gas mark 6 for 10 mins then reduce to 180°C, gas mark 4 for a further 10–15 mins until set.

Makes about 12 tarts. Serve hot or cold. When cold are good in packed lunches.

Orange Soufflé

Ingredients

4 large oranges
100 g sugar
2 eggs, separated
few drops vanilla

Method

1 Cut tops off oranges and remove all the flesh — ensure the skin 'cases' are totally dry.

2 Finely grate the rind from the removed tops.

3 Discard pips and blend orange pulp in a blender or food processor.

4 Strain into a small saucepan, boil for 3–4 mins to reduce the liquid to 80 ml.

5 Add sugar and dissolve in hot liquid then allow to cool.

6 Beat yolks and rind into liquid.

7 Beat whites until stiff.

8 Gently fold the orange mixture into the whites.

9 Fill into orange-skin shells.

10 Place carefully on middle shelf of oven — straight on bars not on a tray.

11 Bake at 180°C, gas mark 4 for 15 mins. Serve immediately.

Serves 4.

Pears Ruby

Ingredients

4 canned pear halves (with no added sugar) *or 2*
whole fresh pears
pinch of ground cloves
¼ tsp cinnamon
½ packet red jelly crystals
200 ml pear juice
4 small scoops ice-cream

Method

1 Place pears in a shallow baking dish and sprinkle
   with the cloves and cinnamon (if using fresh pears,
   peel and core and simmer gently for 10 mins in
   enough water to cover then put in baking dish).

2 Spread jelly crystals evenly over pears.

3 Pour pear juice over pears.

4 Bake at 180°C, gas mark 4 for 15–20 mins basting
   once or twice during cooking.

5 Serve warm with a scoop of ice-cream on top of
   each pear.

Serves 4.

Meal Patterns

Meals do not necessarily follow a set pattern
throughout the world because food
preferences vary according to food needs,
customs and the kind of meal. For example:

- **Food needs**: Diabetics need *portion*
  meals, not three main meals a day. Infants
  take some time to adjust to family meal
  patterns. In third world countries hunger or
  food availability indicate meal times.

- **Customs**: Dairy farming families might
  have four to five meals each day. German
  and Austrian people have Christmas dinner
  late on Christmas Eve.

- **Meal type**: The way in which we might
  serve and eat our evening meal will vary a
  great deal from family to family and
  function to function. Evening Meal might
  be eaten on the knee in front of the
  television, at a meal table, at a formal
  banquet, etc. Foods *we* eat for breakfast are
  not necessarily the same as those eaten in
  other countries.

Just as meal patterns differ, so do the ways
in which foods are served.

- Discuss how an attractive table and
  appetising food may aid in making
  mealtime a time of relaxation, conversation
  and enjoyment.

- Discuss that the dining area can be
  attractive whether the family eats in the
  lounge, dining room, or kitchen.

Wherever or whenever a meal is eaten,
there are usually implements of some
description provided for eating the food, for
example, plates, spoons, forks and chopsticks.

One further element of the meal is
manners. Ever since you were young you
have been told how to behave in different
places and at different times; mealtimes are no
exception. Think back to the discussions
about values in Chapter 1.

- How do you think parents' values might
  influence the manners that they teach their
  children?

- Do you have different rules for meals if
  visitors are present at your home? Discuss
  the reasons why. Can you identify the
  values that influence your behaviour at
  these times?

Why do we bother about manners at all?
Simply because it makes mixing with other
people easier and more pleasant and because
we value what others think of us.

Writing Invitations

Informal invitations are frequently made
inviting people to various functions. These
might be made orally in person, over the
phone or to a group. Sometimes an occasion
to celebrate is considered very special and a
formal invitation requesting a formal reply is
sent. An invitation must give the intended

guest all the details of the occasion that are necessary to make a decision about the reply. This should include:

- the reason for the celebration or party,
- the venue (that is, where it is to be held),
- the date,
- the time,
- when the reply is required,
- sometimes it also tells you whether the dress required is formal or casual. (Formal for men means a collar and tie with a suit, for women it usually means a suitable dress.)

Example:

Invitation
Mr and Mrs K. Tsang
request the pleasure of the company of
Mr John Pleasant
at the twenty-first birthday party of
their daughter Suzanne
on 4th June at the Golden Dragon Restaurant
12 Broad Street, Holton
at 8 pm
RSVP 25th May.

There are also other kinds of invitations. See if you have any at home that you can bring and share with the class.

The letters RSVP tell you that a reply is required. The letters stand for the French words *respondez s'il vous plait* 'reply if you please'. An example of a reply to the above example invitation would be:

Mr John Pleasant has much
pleasure in accepting the kind
invitation of Mr and Mrs K. Tsang
to attend the twenty-first
birthday party of their daughter
Suzanne on 4th June.

34 Church Street
Frazerton

Note that the reply is not written as a normal letter but in the same vein as the invitation.

Workshop

1 Serve foods in as many different ways as possible to give yourself the opportunity to practise different ways of eating.

2 Have a table setting and/or a serviette folding competition at school and prepare and serve a formal meal for the winners.

3 Prepare a formal invitation inviting a friend, teacher or relative to a meal or afternoon tea in the Home Economics Room. Plan the menu for the occasion and attend to your guests on the special day.

4 See if you can organise an outing to a restaurant as a class activity or end of term party.

Part 4

◇

Finding Out About Shelter

8 Meeting Shelter Needs

In the early chapters of this book we looked at the basic needs of human beings. Food and shelter were ranked as being two of the most important, or certainly two on which the family concentrates large amounts of time, energy and money.

This chapter will concentrate on exploring how our housing needs are met in today's society.

Workshop

1 **Housing Needs**
   a Draw or sketch a plan of your house.
   b On each room note what happens in that room.
   c List the *needs* that you feel are being satisfied by the activities carried out in each room.
   d Share your ideas with another person. Make a list of the needs being met in the house.
   e As a class discuss your findings and draw up a list of the needs that are met within a house.

2 **Housing and Resources**
   The ways our needs are met through housing are affected by the resources we have available to use.
   a Identify and discuss what resources affect the choice of a home.
   b Look at housing in the area surrounding your school.
      — What environmental factors (weather patterns, terrain, historic value) do you think were considered when these homes were built?
      — What do you think determined the types of building materials in each home?
      — Why is it more likely that a house in the country may have an open wood fire than a house in the city?

3 **Housing and History**
   The ways housing needs have been met have varied over the years. Housing provides us with an insight into the period in which a particular type of architecture or building material was used.
   a Opposite are pictures of houses commonly seen in this country. Using the libraries available to you, research the period in history

when the type of architecture represented in each of these houses
was popular. Write a paragraph about each period of time
describing day-to-day living.

b Discuss the building materials used, architectural style and the type
of family that might have lived in each type of house.

Investigation No. 22
Housing

Housing throughout history has been designed to meet the needs of people; needs such as shelter, protection, comfort, cooking and storage of food.

Aim

- To compare the way housing met the needs of a family in the 1850s with housing today.

Procedure

a Revise the list of family housing needs compiled in activity 1 of the workshop above.

b Visit a historical house built around 1850. Contact your local historical society or the National Trust for information about historic homes in your area. Alternatively, view a video on housing in the 1850s.

   This exercise could be adapted to coincide with the period being studied by the pupils in history lessons.

c Find out how the housing needs on your list were met in the 1850s. Record your answers.

d Compare the meeting of needs in 1850 with how needs are met in your own home.

Discussion/Conclusion

e Discuss your data. Have the needs of a family changed over that time (for example, the outbuildings, the schoolroom, the kitchen)? In what ways have they changed? What could have caused these changes? How does the modern home differ? In what ways is it similar?

f Draw your conclusions. In what ways do houses meet the needs of individuals?

Meeting Today's Housing Needs

People select different types of housing; housing that best suits their needs in today's society. The following types of housing are commonly found in this country.
—Detached houses
—Flats and maisonettes
—Terraced houses and town houses
—Semi Detached houses.
—Mobile homes

- Discuss what factors would, or could, influence the type of home a person would select.

Obtaining a Home

People are faced with two choices when looking for a home:

- renting
- buying.

Detached house

Flats and Maisonettes

Bungalow

Semi detached house

Terraced house

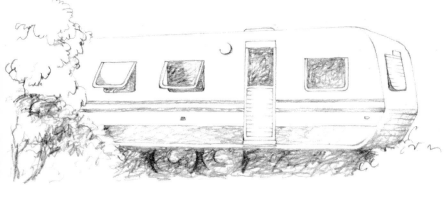

Mobile home

Workshop

1 Contact a local citizens advice bureau or housing department to find out how you would go about renting a home.

2 Look at the property advertisements in the local paper. Find out about the type of property for sale in the area where you live.

3 Every week the daily papers have many advertisements for houses. Look at the advertisements below.
   a What abbreviations are used? What do they stand for?
   b Write in your own words a brief description of each of the houses advertised.
   c Imagine that you are putting your present home up for sale. Write a suitable advertisement for the daily paper.

Excellent modernised gas ch 3 bed palisaded terr house. Carpets incl. Viewing recomm.

Sycamore Road
Refurbished and ext 2 bed det bung, car stdg and rear gdns.

99 Main Street
Det hse in convnt loc, 2 recep, 4 bed, fitted brkfst kit, d/gge. Tel: 416776.

Excellent 3 bed part ch semi. Garage space, garden.

Well appt 2 bed ground floor flat, gfch, d/glaz, brick gge, easy walking distance town centre.

Good 3 bed modern det property in pleasant location convenient for all amenities. Porch, hall, lnge, dining, kit, bathrm, gas ch, d/glazing, gge/workshop, private gdns, carpets and curtains included.

18 The Green
Spac 3 bed semi, lnge/din, brkfst kit, bathrm/shwr, warm air htg. internal viewing recomm.

Spac 3 bed twn hse, lge lnge, din rm, kit, gge, car stdg space.

Deciding Where

Where a family chooses to live relates to:

- Family mobility — the jobs of family members can mean limited time in any one place.
- The family life cycle — the age of the children.
- Income — the amount of money the family has to spend on housing.
- Family values — different families will place differing values on the importance of housing, and the type of housing the family wants.
- Community resources — the proximity of schools, hospitals, employment, etc. may also influence where people choose to live.

Whether families rent or buy their homes will also be influenced by many of the above points.

Case Study

Sally and Anna are both 18 and have just left school. They have decided to move to the city to look for employment. This decision means that they have to find somewhere to live. This is how they go about it.

Problem — Where to live?
Decisions to make

- How much can be spent?
  Sally discovers that the rent of the flat is not the only expense involved. Rent does not

over electricity and gas payments, a month's rent has to be paid in advance, as a deposit. (A deposit is money paid to the agent or owner. It is usually the equivalent of one or two month's rent. The agent invests this and it is returned when the house or flat is vacated, as long as it is in the same condition as it was at the start of the lease.)

What type of accommodation is needed? A flat? A house? A bedsitter? A bungalow?

Sally and Anna have to decide what their needs are and work out issues such as should they share a room or not? What size space do they need? How much privacy do they want? Are there any other issues they need to consider?

Should the accommodation be close to work, public transport, shops, etc? This may depend on fare costs, whether they have a car or not, the time they are prepared to spend daily on travel — travel costs to work add to living expenses.

Should the accommodation be furnished or unfurnished?

• Where to look for the accommodation? Sally and Anna draw up the following list. Can it be added to ?

— Daily papers, especially mid-week and Saturday.
— Some local councils have accommodation officers.
— The Citizens Advice Bureau might be able to assist.
— Noticeboards at universities, colleges and some shopping centres also advertise.

Answering the above questions will help Sally and Anna to develop a clear idea of what they want and what they can afford. This will be helpful to ensure that they are not pressured into anything that they don't want.

The next steps in obtaining their accommodation will be as follows:

Inspection of the available accommodation (carrying a checklist of what is needed is helpful). When inspecting the accommodation they should check that everything is working: taps, toilets, cooker, security of doors and windows, etc.

• A decision on accommodation.
• A list should be made of any faults that they may be blamed for later, for example, dirty walls or carpet or cracked windows. They will have to reach specific agreement with the owner or agent as to the condition of the premises, as a check for deposit repayment when moving out.

General points Sally and Anna have to consider:

• They may have to sign a tenancy agreement which gives details of their rights and responsibilities as tenants, this should be studied carefully. They should get advice from a solicitor or the Citizens Advice Bureau if they do not understand the agreement.

Families Renting

Not only single people rent. Many families find renting suits their needs, for some or all of the following reasons:

• not tied to a job because of house repayments
• more flexibility and adaptability possible in regard to health or changes in the family
• permits moving to a more expensive or less expensive house if the income changes
• permits moving if there is a promotion or change in work requiring a move
• permits moving to adjust to an expanding or contracting family
• no depletion in family funds to pay a deposit
• no responsibility or worry related to taxes, insurance and repairs
• no long-term indebtedness

- provides experiences which may help one judge a house when buying (in relation to size, room relationship, site and location, heating, plumbing, size of garden, etc.)
- may be obtained furnished when investment in furniture is not desired.

Discuss and compile a list of points against renting accommodation.

Buying a Home

Most people choose to buy their own home if they are able to.

Owning your own home is seen as desirable because:

- the family has a house to show for the payments
- home ownership helps to provide a feeling of security
- the responsibility of ownership in meeting rates and other property charges as well as repaying the housing loan helps to develop business judgement and skill as well as a sense of responsibility toward the family
- the home owner has greater freedom in relation to decisions about the property, for example, extensions and alterations
- there is an opportunity for freedom of expression and activity

Buying a home is usually the largest single financial investment most people ever make. Because of the money involved, it is important that people make informed decisions on obtaining mortgages and on purchasing a home.

Some points you should investigate are:

- your legal responsibilities
- hidden costs
- insurance

It is advisable when buying a home to employ a solicitor or qualified conveyancer to deal with the legal side of the sale such as the drawing up of contracts and the transfer of money.

The following points should be considered when choosing a home:

- Location — is it close to community resources, schools, public transport, employment, etc?
- Environment — does it provide protection from the elements, privacy, a safe and healthy environment free of hazards as we as space for production, recreation and leisure activities?
- Type of Home — is the layout and design the house suitable for the purchasers? Do th number and sizes of the rooms meet their needs? Is the house structurally sound? Ar the roof, walls and windows in good condition? Are the plumbing, electrics and heating in good repair?

Meeting Food Preparation Needs in the Home

Because much of our life is concerned with meeting our food needs, the food preparatio centre of any home is important.

- What happens in your kitchen at home? Is food preparation the only thing that happens? Discuss.

Although the kitchen is one of the smaller rooms in the house it is probably used more than any other. It must therefore be a manageable space.

Kitchens can be generally classified into the space shapes shown in the diagram p. 187.

No matter which way a kitchen is planned the movement between the sink, the cooker and the refrigerator, that is, the *work triangle*, should be kept to a workable level. There should be little or no traffic through the work triangle.

- Why is this important?
- which do you think is the most manageable work triangle?

Surfaces should be easy to clean with as few joins as possible to minimise bacteria breeding areas. The room should be well-lit s work can be carried out safely. Storage areas or utensils and food should be adequate and easily cleaned as well as easily reached.

Food preparation areas are needed beside the stove and the sink, and, if possible, beside the refrigerator (food preparation is, after all, the main reason for having a kitchen). Adequate ventilation is a must.

- Can you think of reasons for this?

A table and chairs and/or bench and stools might be included where there is space. Colour selection for all surfaces should emphasise colours that are 'livable'. Too many very bright colours can be overpowering.

Basic Kitchen Shapes

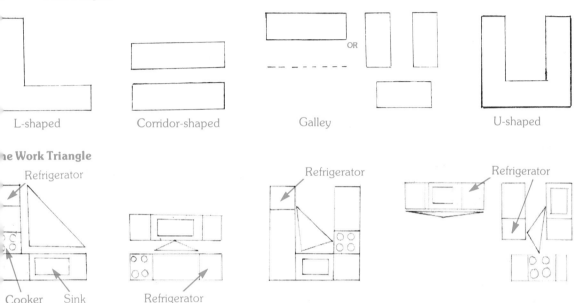

L-shaped   Corridor-shaped   Galley   U-shaped

The Work Triangle

Refrigerator   Refrigerator   Refrigerator

Cooker   Sink   Refrigerator

Workshop

a   Look at the house plans on the next page
Which house is the most appropriate for a family with four children?
Which house is the most appropriate for a young childless couple?
Which house is the most appropriate for an elderly retired couple?
Which house is the most appropriate for a family with two children?

b   Give reasons for all your choices above.

a   Visit show homes or a kitchen planning area, for example, a commercial kitchen fitter, or the gas or electricity showroom display area. Discover the main considerations for kitchen planning.

b   Plan a kitchen. Copy the diagram on page 190 on to a piece of paper and draw the shape of your ideal kitchen on the grid—extend to another piece of paper if necessary. Mark the positions of doors and windows. Select major fittings from the scale drawings above the grid (there is a variety of sizes in appliances and sinks and 600 mm deep base units). Trace over your choices, cut them out and fit them on to your kitchen layout, remembering that their positions might involve plumbing and power. Allow room for doors to swing and try to avoid traffic areas being through the work triangle. Indicate eye-level (overhead) cupboards and shelves with dotted lines and halve or square the table if desired.

c Write a complete description of your planned kitchen including colours, type of surfaces on floor, walls, cupboards and worktops, lighting, window aspect, window treatment and so on.

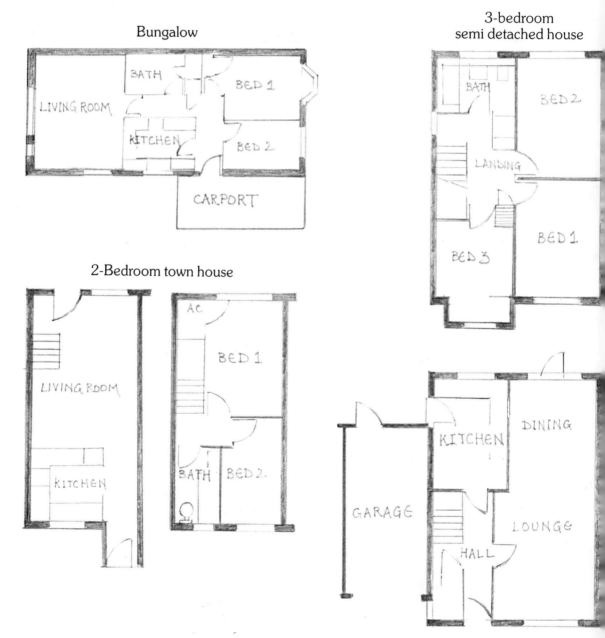

Bungalow

3-bedroom
semi detached house

2-Bedroom town house

4-Bedroom semi detached house

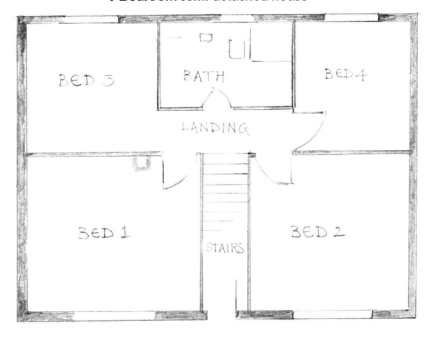

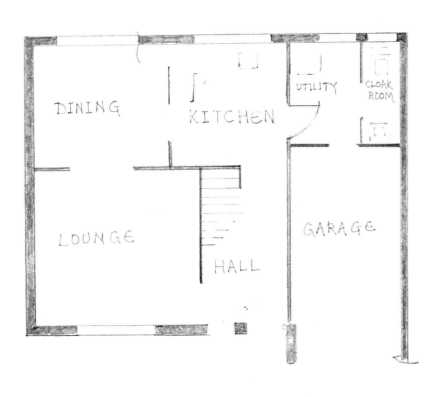

Kitchen Planner

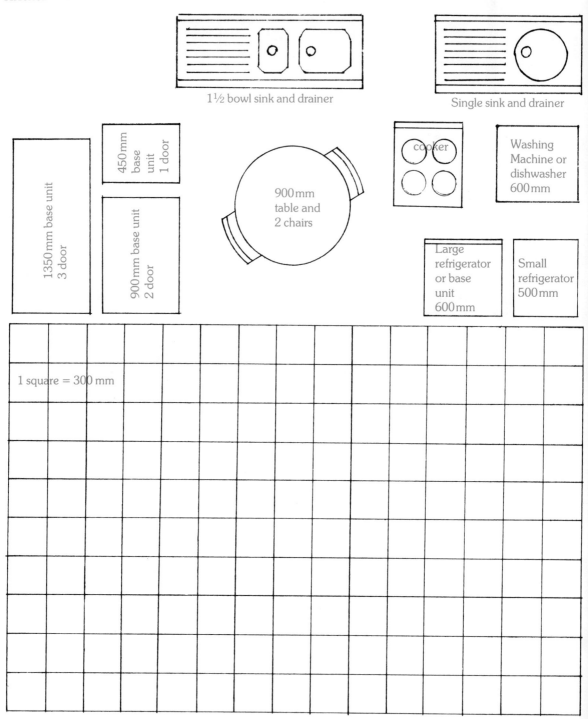

1½ bowl sink and drainer

Single sink and drainer

450 mm base unit 1 door

1350 mm base unit 3 door

900 mm base unit 2 door

900 mm table and 2 chairs

cooker

Washing Machine or dishwasher 600 mm

Large refrigerator or base unit 600 mm

Small refrigerator 500 mm

1 square = 300 mm

5 **Case Study A**

Mr and Mrs McKenzie have three children, a son Karl aged 18, who is studying at university, a daughter Suzy, aged 14, and a son Sam, aged 8.

They are concerned that their present home is inadequate to meet their needs. They have investigated enlarging their house but this is not practical, so they are going to buy a new home.

Karl has a car, so travel to university is not a problem. Mr McKenzie is self-employed and in his spare time restores old cars. Mrs McKenzie likes to spend several hours gardening each day. Karl wants a room of his own or a quiet study as he finds it difficult to study in the present home.

Mrs McKenzie enjoys walking and would like to be able to walk to the shops. Suzy is a good athlete and trains daily. Both Suzy and Sam are still at school.

Draw up a check-list, in order of importance, that the McKenzies could use as a guide when looking for a new house.

6 **Case Study B**

Joe and Mark have been renting a flat for the last six months. Joe is feeling disappointed about the arrangement, he is keen to study and do well at his course. Mark just wants to socialise every night.

Sharing accommodation can often cause problems like this. Discuss how this conflict situation could be solved.

7 **Case Study C**

Mary and Peter have just been married. They have £3000 saved and are unsure about whether to rent or buy a home. Peter is a mechanic and at present works at a local garage. He plans to buy a garage of his own at a later stage. He works long hours, six days a week. Mary is a nurse; she works shift work and hopes to continue with her work for a number of years.

Discuss with Mary and Peter the advantages and disadvantages of renting. Make a recommendation to them as to what you think they should do.

8 *What Is It?*

   a Although it is relatively small it must be a very well planned manageable space. It is often called the centre of the home.
   b It often has to be signed by a tenant. It includes the rules of tenancy and should not have any blank spaces when it is signed.
   c It usually has to be paid before a rented place is occupied. It is part of an agreement between tenant and landlord. It can be redeemed.
   d It is the area between three heavily used areas. It is best if there is very little traffic passing through it.

Puzzle

Identify the eight home economics words
represented by the diagrams below.

Appendix

Process Chart

Explanation of symbols used:

○ Means that something is being *moved*, for example, a saucepan from the cupboard to the stove.

○ Means that an object is being *changed*, for example, chopping parsley or peeling the shell from a hard-boiled egg.

☐ Means that *checking* is occurring, for example, an ingredient is being measured or ingredients simmering in a saucepan are being checked.

▽ Means that there is a *delay* in activity, for example, waiting for fat to heat.

Steps	Movement	Change	Checking	Delay or Storage	Description of Method
	○	○	☐	▽	
	○	○	☐	▽	
	○	○	☐	▽	
	○	○	☐	▽	
	○	○	☐	▽	
	○	○	☐	▽	
	○	○	☐	▽	
	○	○	☐	▽	
	○	○	☐	▽	
	○	○	☐	▽	
	○	○	☐	▽	
	○	○	☐	▽	
	○	○	☐	▽	
	○	○	☐	▽	
	○	○	☐	▽	
	○	○	☐	▽	
	○	○	☐	▽	
	○	○	☐	▽	
	○	○	☐	▽	
	○	○	☐	▽	

Steps	Movement	Change	Checking	Delay or Storage	Description of Method
○	◯	□	▽		
○	◯	□	▽		
○	◯	□	▽		
○	◯	□	▽		
○	◯	□	▽		
○	◯	□	▽		
○	◯	□	▽		
○	◯	□	▽		
○	◯	□	▽		
○	◯	□	▽		
○	◯	□	▽		
○	◯	□	▽		
○	◯	□	▽		
○	◯	□	▽		
○	◯	□	▽		
○	◯	□	▽		
○	◯	□	▽		
○	◯	□	▽		
○	◯	□	▽		
○	◯	□	▽		
○	◯	□	▽		
○	◯	□	▽		
○	◯	□	▽		
○	◯	□	▽		
○	◯	□	▽		
○	◯	□	▽		
○	◯	□	▽		
○	◯	□	▽		

Puzzle Answers

Chapter 4 p. 77 Workshop activity
Protein

Chapter 4 p. 98 Workshop activity

body	food	natural
bran	fresh	prescribed
check	function	regimen
composition	habitual	skin
course	health	stamina
daily	heart	substance
dietitian	healthy	vital
dietetics	iron	vitality
endure	lungs	way
energy	malnutrition	will
essential	meat	wheatgerm
exercise	medical	
feed	minerals	

Chapter 5 p. 116 Workshop activity
Vegetable Crossword

Across:

1 bag
3 rot
5 raw
7 pan
8 marrow
12 leafy
14 aim
15 pea
16 water
17 endive
18 swede
19 onion

Down:

1 beetroot
2 yam
3 raw
4 on
6 waxy
7 potato
9 pumpkin
10 bean
11 parsnip
12 leeks
13 fried
16 wet

Chapter 5 p. 125 Fruit and Vegetable Puzzle

apple	chicory	lettuce
artichoke	cos	melon
asparagus	cress	pea
aubergine	cucumber	peach
broccoli	fig	pear
cabbage	grapes	plum
cauliflower	leek	potato
celery	lemon	quince
cherry		swede

Chapter 5 p. 128 Workshop activity
4 What is it?

a vitamin C
b calcium
c microwave oven
d carrot
e cabbage
f iron
g baking
h apple
i basal metabolic rate
j lamb

Chapter 5 p. 133 Workshop activity

Cereal

Chapter 5 p. 147–148 Food Puzzles

1 bread
   cream
   knead
   steak
   yeast
   feast

2 meat
   pea
   bean
   sear
   veal
   pheasant
   leaf
   steam

3 1 cabbage (cab/age)
   2 lettuce (let/us)
   3 butter (butt/er)
   4 stew
   5 carrot (car/rot)
   6 chop
   7 steak (stake)
   8 jam
   9 potatoes (pot/a/toes)
   10 raisin (ray/sin)

4 *Across:*

2 veal
4 protein
6 mug
7 meat
9 grills
12 one
14 cane
15 eat

Down:

1 caring
2 vitamin
3 animal
5 nuts
8 elect
10 root
11 rye
13 pea

Chapter 6 p. 159 Crazy Puzzle

Across:	*Down:*
2 bread	1 cake
3 berries	4 soup
5 pies	5 peas
7 flour	6 salt
9 pineapple	8 rice
11 cereal	10 scone
14 nut	12 lemon
15 meat	13 fat

Chapter 6 p. 160 What is it?

a resources	f communication signals
b values	g a family
c evaluation	h myself
d process chart	i food
e the problem	j convection oven

Chapter 7 p.172 Food Puzzle

brawn, bun, cake, chips, chops, cream, goose, honey, jam, leek, loaf, nuts, toast, trifle, tripe, turkey.

Chapter 8 p. 168 Workshop activity—What am I?

a the kitchen
b a lease
c a bond
d the work triangle

Chapter 8 p. 192 Puzzle

1 housing (how/sing)
2 management (man/age/men/t)
3 saucepan (sauce/pan)
4 fold
5 nutrition (nut(s)/(w)rit(e)/i(r)on)
6 knead (kneed)
7 marinade (marina/de)
8 sauté (saw/t(r)ay)

Glossary

Management Terms

Decision-making selecting from alternatives

Goals aims, or those things we wish to achieve in our lives

Needs primary — resources that you need to stay alive
secondary — social resources that make us feel a whole person

Resources the things that you use to obtain your goals

Standards the guides used to measure success in achieving your goals.

Wants desires, or those things that are not essential for your survival, but you would like to have

Values the beliefs that you hold

Food Preparation Terms

Au Gratin food covered with sauce, sprinkled with crumbs or grated cheese, dotted with butter and browned under the grill

Bake cook by dry heat in an oven

Beating mixing food to introduce air

Blending combining ingredients with a spoon, beater, or blender to achieve a smooth mixture

Blini pancake made of buckwheat and yeast

Boiling cooking in liquid at 100°C

Casserole a   cook pot complete with lid
b   a slow cooked stew of meat, fish or vegetables

Chop to cut into very small pieces with a sharp knife or chopper

Cream to beat butter/margarine and sugar to a light creamy consistency about twice its original volume

Crêpe a thin pancake

Dice cut into cubes

Duchess puréed potato piped into a set shape

Frites fried

Folding-in enveloping one ingredient or mixture in another using a large metal spoon or spatula

Garnishing decorating a dish with edible decorations

Grate to rub food against a grater to form small particles

Glaze a glossy finish given to food by brushing with beaten egg, milk or sugar syrup

Grill to cook by direct heat such as an open fire, charcoal, gas or electricity

Gnocchi small dumplings made from potato, semolina or choux pastry

Kebab meat cubes marinaded and grilled on a skewer

Marinade blend of oil, wine or vinegar, herbs and spices used to flavour and tenderise meat

Noisette a cut of lamb from the best end of neck, boned, trimmed and tied with string into a small round

Pasta paste made from flour and water — group name given to spaghetti, macaroni, etc.

Pommes French for potatoes

Purée sieved raw or cooked food

Ramekin individual baking dish

Rissole a small patty usually made from cooked ground or minced meat

Sauté to fry food rapidly in shallow, hot fat, tossing and turning until evenly browned

Seasoning salt, pepper, spices or herbs, which are added to food to improve flavour

Soufflé a dish consisting of a sauce or purée which is thickened with egg yolks into which stiffly beaten eggwhites are folded

Stewing to simmer food slowly in a covered pan or casserole

Strudel thin leaves of pastry filled with fruit, nuts or savoury mixtures which are rolled and baked

Recipe Index

Subject Index

REVIEW FORM

How have you used this Text?
(Tick one box only)

☐ Home study

☐ On a course_____

☐ Other _____

Why did you decide to purchase this Text? *(Tick one box only)*

☐ Have used BPP Texts in the past

☐ Recommendation by friend/colleague

☐ Recommendation by a college lecturer

☐ Saw advertising

☐ Other _____

During the past six months do you recall seeing/receiving either of the following?
(Tick as many boxes as are relevant)

☐ Our advertisement in Accounting Technician

☐ Our Publishing Catalogue

Which (if any) aspects of our advertising do you think are useful?
(Tick as many boxes as are relevant)

☐ Prices and publication dates of new editions

☐ Information on Text content

☐ Details of our free online offering

☐ None of the above

Your ratings, comments and suggestions would be appreciated on the following areas of this Text.

	Very useful	Useful	Not useful
Introductory section	☐	☐	☐
Quality of explanations	☐	☐	☐
How it works	☐	☐	☐
Chapter tasks	☐	☐	☐
Chapter Overviews	☐	☐	☐
Test your learning	☐	☐	☐
Index	☐	☐	☐

	Excellent	Good	Adequate	Poor
Overall opinion of this Text	☐	☐	☐	☐

Do you intend to continue using BPP Products?　　☐ Yes　　☐ No

Please note any further comments and suggestions/errors on the reverse of this page. The author of this edition can be e-mailed at: paulsutcliffe@bpp.com

Please return to: Paul Sutcliffe, Senior Publishing Manager, BPP Learning Media Ltd, FREEPOST, London, W12 8BR.

REVIEW FORM (continued)

TELL US WHAT YOU THINK

Please note any further comments and suggestions/errors below.